D0205933

ST. GREGORY OF NYSSA

THE LORD'S PRAYER
THE BEATITUDES

Ancient Christian Writers

THE WORKS OF THE FATHERS IN TRANSLATION

EDITED BY

JOHANNES QUASTEN, S. T. D.
*Professor of Ancient Church History
and Christian Archaeology*

JOSEPH C. PLUMPE, Ph. D.
*Professor of Patristic Greek
and Ecclesiastical Latin*

The Catholic University of America
Washington, D. C.

No. 18

ST. GREGORY OF NYSSA

THE LORD'S PRAYER

THE BEATITUDES

TRANSLATED AND ANNOTATED

BY

HILDA C. GRAEF

Senior Assistant
Oxford Lexicon of Patristic Greek

PAULIST PRESS

New York / Mahwah

Nihil Obstat:

        J. Quasten
          Cens. Dep.

Imprimatur:

        Patricius A. O'Boyle, D.D.
          Archiep. Washingtonen.
            die 10 Dec. 1953

Library of Congress
Catalog Card Number: 78-62466

ISBN: 0-8091-0255-2

PUBLISHED BY PAULIST PRESS
997 Macarthur Blvd.
Mahwah, NJ 07430

PRINTED AND BOUND IN THE UNITED STATES OF AMERICA

CONTENTS

ST. GREGORY OF NYSSA

THE LORD'S PRAYER
THE BEATITUDES

INTRODUCTION

Gregory of Nyssa has long been neglected by Patristic scholars, as is evident from the lack both of an adequate critical edition and of translations of his works. Only recently has he begun to attract attention; we need but mention the names of Professor Werner Jaeger of Harvard and of Père Daniélou. This long obscurity is not altogether inexplicable. Gregory of Nyssa was neither a great bishop and monastic legislator like his brother, St. Basil the Great, nor an attractive preacher and poet like his friend, Gregory of Nazianzus, the third of the three great Cappadocians, as they are generally called. He was a speculative theologian and a mystic, whose orthodoxy, though recognized by the Second Council of Nicea (787), was yet slightly suspect owing to a tinge of Origenism, so that he was never admitted to the select circle of the great doctors such as St. Athanasius, St. Basil himself, St. Chrysostom, or St. John of Damascus.

Of his life we know comparatively little. He was born about the year 335, and, as he himself tells us in a letter,[1] was educated chiefly by his elder brother Basil, with whom he was united by a lifelong friendship. Like him he wanted to become a priest. He had already been made a lector, when he abandoned this plan in order to embrace the career of rhetor. He seems almost certainly to have been married; for in his treatise on virginity[2] there occurs a passage in which he regrets that he himself is prevented from attaining to the glory of this virtue. Moreover, in a letter of his friend and namesake of Nazianzus [3] the death of a certain Theosebia is mentioned in terms which strongly suggest that she was Gregory's wife, though the Maurist editors of Gregory of Nazianzus' works would make her out to have been a deaconess.

However this may be, his brother and his friends succeeded in weaning him from his worldly ambitions. Having given up his career as a rhetor, he probably first went to a monastic foundation his brother had made in Pontus, where he practised the ascetic life and studied theology. In 371 Basil appointed him bishop of Nyssa, a small town in Basil's own metropolitan district of Caesarea in Cappadocia. Though his episcopal duties in this tiny diocese cannot have been very strenuous, his lack of firmness with people and of prudence especially in financial matters drew upon him the reproaches of his brother.[4] His determined adherence to the Nicene faith, moreover, made him suspect to the pro-Arian government. In 376 a synod, attended chiefly by Arian bishops and court prelates, met at Nyssa and deposed him in his absence. Gregory had to flee his diocese, but after the death of the Arian Emperor Valens (378) he returned to his see and was given a triumphal reception.

In the meantime his theological writings had earned him a high reputation. He attended the Synod of Antioch in 379, and, much against his will, was elected archbishop of Sebaste (380), which he administered for a few months. He was one of the foremost theologians who defended the orthodox faith at the Council of Constantinople in 381. He was evidently also highly esteemed at the court of that city; for he was chosen to preach the funeral orations both for the princess Pulcheria, in 385 or 386, and for her mother, the empress Flaccilla, who died soon afterwards. He himself died about the year 394.

Gregory of Nyssa took an active part in combating the great heresies of his time. His treatise *Contra Eunomium*, now happily available in the critical edition of Professor Jaeger, is a brilliant refutation of Eunomius, a most violent protagonist of the Arian heresy. It was written in defence of his brother Basil, who had himself published a treatise against Eunomius and had been viciously attacked by him. In the *Contra Apollinarem* he vigorously refutes the two Apollinarian theses that the flesh of Christ had descended from Heaven, and that in Him the Word took the place of the human mind (νοῦς). Besides these he devoted a number of minor writings to the refutation of the heresiarchs.

His most important dogmatic work is the *Oratio catechetica*. It is an exposition of the principal doctrines of the Catholic faith—the Trinity, the Incarnation, the Redemption, and the Sacraments of Baptism and the Eucharist. His ideas on the origin of man, the destiny of the soul, and the resurrection of the body are developed especially in *De hominis opificio* and *De anima et resurrectione*. The latter, in the form of a dialogue dedicated to the memory of his sister Macrina the Younger, is modelled on Plato's *Phaido*. But the fulness of the Christian faith in the immortality of the soul and the resurrection of the body gave the work of the later author, despite its inferior literary quality, a far greater depth and beauty than the pagan philosopher could achieve. At the same time it must be admitted that it is here, in his treatment of the last things, that the influence of his revered master Origen is most noticeable, and actually caused him to swerve from the straight path of orthodoxy. Though Gregory never admitted the great Alexandrian's speculations on the pre-existence and migration of souls, he shared his doctrine of ἀποκατάστασις, which denies the eternity of hell and believes in an ultimate restoration of all, including the devil, to the vision of God.

It is only in recent times that Gregory of Nyssa has been rediscovered as an ascetical and mystical writer of the highest importance; witness the brilliant study which Père Daniélou devoted to this side of his work, entitled *Platonisme et contemplation mystique*.

The spiritual doctrine of the great Cappadocian is embodied chiefly in his *De virginitate*, which elaborates the thesis that virginity makes the soul the bride of Christ, and in a series of exegetical works. In these the influence of Origen, who so often sacrificed the literal sense of a passage to his allegorical-mystical speculations, is paramount. In the *De vita Moysis* Gregory interprets the life of the Israelite lawgiver in terms of the ascent of the soul to union with God. In the two books on the titles of the Psalms he develops the idea that the five books of Psalms form as many steps on the ladder leading to perfection, a notion we meet again in his treatise on the Beatitudes. This conception of the spiritual life as a ladder became a favourite with later ascetical writers, and found its most famous expression in the *Scala Paradisi* of St. John Climacus. The same trend of thought permeates also his homilies on Ecclesiastes, which in his view has for its object to elevate the soul above the world of the senses. Mystical exegesis naturally reaches its summit in his homilies on the Canticles, which to him represent the union of love between God and the soul. This had also been the view of Origen, whose exegesis of the Canticles Gregory praises in his own work, and this interpretation has been accepted by all mystical theologians since.

Compared with these great works of mystical exegesis, the present two series of homilies, on the Lord's Prayer and on the Beatitudes, are far more in the nature of real homilies, hence more concerned with moral exhortation than with allegorical interpretation, though the latter is not altogether absent; in fact, such favourite ideas of Gregory as the mystical significance of the Holy of Holies and the restoration of the dimmed Image of God in man to its original splendour occur frequently also in these two minor works. One of their most striking characteristics is that they are intensely practical, and full of highly coloured examples not only from the moral and social life, but also from the medical and scientific thought of his time. This latter is, indeed, a remarkable feature of Gregory's writings, due no doubt to his thorough training, during his career as rhetor, in the classical authors as well as in contemporary culture. In fact, his mystical theology rests on a solid basis not only of sound dogmatic theology, but also of a wide acquaintance with ordinary human life and non-theological scholarship, which is as characteristic of him as it is of his brother Basil.

The treatise on the Lord's Prayer begins with an introduction on the need for prayer and its neglect by most Christians, which reads almost as if it were written for our own time. Already in this first sermon a favourite theme of Gregory's mystic teaching is sounded, one that has already been mentioned: the theme of the Divine Image in which the soul was made, which was tarnished by sin and is to be restored to its original beauty. In order to recover this beauty, man must learn to pray aright and for the right things. The following four sermons deal with the various petitions of the Our Father one by one, castigating the vices of his time, especially greed for riches and gluttony, which were particularly rampant in the Byzantine Empire. Every now and again, however, Gregory leaves the strictly moral sphere and takes flight into the realm of Divine Beauty. It is during such excursions that his exegesis here, too, sometimes leaves altogether the firm ground of the literal sense and loses itself in "mystical" interpretation which the modern reader, untrained in the school of Alexandrian theology, may sometimes find difficult to follow. But happily these flights of allegory are not too frequent in the present two works. In general Gregory has in view the needs of the average Christian, which, on closer acquaintance with his writings, strike one as having remained much the same after the 1600 years that separate his time from our own.

Towards the end of the third Sermon there is a doctrinally important passage on the Trinity, which for some reason or other has dropped out of a number of manuscripts and is also missing from the editions. Migne's Patrology (MG 46.1109) gives part of it among the fragments. It was first published by Cardinal Mai as a section of the third Sermon on the Lord's Prayer, and again later in his *Nova Patrum Bibl.*[4] (Rome 1947) as *Fragmentum de processione Spiritus Sancti etiam a Filio.*[5] Krabinger[6] incorporated it in his edition of the Sermons, as did also Oehler.[7] In 1904 K. Holl[8] declared the piece to be a "Western forgery" in the interests of the *Filioque*, without having even touched on the question of the literary and manuscript evidence. He should have seen from Cardinal

Mai's edition, which he used, that the fragment was cited by the *Doctrina Patrum de Verbi incarnatione* as early as 700 A. D. Besides, the Codex Vaticanus graecus 2066 (7th or 8th cent.) contains Gregory's sermon with this passage. In the face of this evidence it is difficult to see how Holl could speak of a "Western forgery."

His principal argument, however, is based on the supposedly "non-Gregorian, partly even non-Greek phrases with which the whole is studded": by these he thought the spuriousness of the fragment could be "palpably" proved. F. Diekamp [9] readily showed that these phrases occurred—sometimes verbatim—in other writings of Gregory of Nyssa, or else had striking parallels in his style and vocabulary. Thus Holl's argumentation collapses. His attempt to show up a doctrinal contrast between the piece and Gregory's other works fares no better. In the former the etiological relationship between the Son and the Holy Spirit is expressed by the Pauline phrase πνεῦμα Χριστοῦ (Rom. 8.9), and Holl adds that it is not only un-Scriptural, but altogether impossible, to reverse the relationship and to call the son Χριστὸς πνεύματος. The author then asserts that Gregory actually wrote what the passage under discussion says to be impossible and adduces *Adversus Macedonium* (MG 45.1321A) as proof. But in this latter passage Gregory says that the Son is χρισθεὶς τῷ πνεύματι, anointed with the Spirit, something totally different from Χριστὸς πνεύματος. Holl seems to have overlooked the fact that Gregory here is not dealing with the etiological relationship, but is concerned with proving the identity of nature (ὁμοουσία) of the Holy Spirit with the Father and the Son. Hence his attempt to prove that the fragment is spurious has failed completely: both the manuscript tradition and the theological contents point to its authenticity.

Gregory was not the first of the Greek Fathers to write an exegetical treatise on the Lord's Prayer. Of Clement of Alexandria we have only a few passages on the subject, scattered among his works, but sufficient to give us an idea of his exegetical views. Origen explained the Our Father in detail in his treatise *On Prayer*, and Cyril of Jerusalem did the same in the fifth of his *Mystagogical Catecheses*. Of later Fathers, St. John Chrysostom interpreted it in his *Commentary on Matthew* (as did Peter of Laodicea) and also in a separate homily. Theodore of Mopsuestia wrote on it in a recently discovered catechesis. Cyril of Alexandria commented it in the version according to St. Luke, and Maximus Confessor wrote a profound treatise on it.

To what extent does Gregory depend on his predecessors, Origen and Cyril of Jerusalem? At first sight the later writer's conception of man as a child of God, developed in the explanation of the address "Our Father," shows much affinity with Origen. Both take the address as expressing man's moral similarity with God. Man is allowed to call God "Father" only if he has purified his life from evil. Hence man's sonship consists in the moral purity of a good conscience, and the opening words of the Prayer are meant to exhort us to a virtuous life. This consequence of the idea of sonship is the same in Origen and Gregory. But it is derived from different premises. Whereas Origen proves it with a wealth of Scriptural citations, Gregory develops it speculatively from the concept of "father" as well as from ethical maxims generally. If a man knows how to appreciate the Divine qualities, he will not dare to call himself a child of God unless he finds these also in himself. In Origen as in Gregory the Divine sonship of the good is opposed to the diabolic sonship of the wicked.

The explanation of the second petition, too, has philosophical discussions in the place of the Biblical considerations of Origen and Cyril. Whereas the earlier writers see in the Kingdom of God (or of Heaven) the definite religious entity proclaimed in the Gospel, Gregory speculates on the concept of βασιλεία. He first refutes an erroneous interpretation which implies that God is not yet King of this Kingdom. He is King of the universe even now, and in any case His immutability would prevent His changing into another state, some new manner of Kingship. Further arguments are modelled on Plato's Republic. Hence he emphasizes especially the factor of power. There is no higher kingdom in the world than God's and it is to be established everywhere, including the moral sphere. But this is to be done by obedience freely given; and it is precisely here that, owing to the First Man's false decision, the hostile forces of sin and death have set up their terrible tyranny. And so the Kingdom of God among men can be initiated only by means of a relentless warfare on the battlefield of the soul. The perfect dominion of God will not be achieved until sin and death have been overcome, in a holy alliance between God and the soul. Gregory, therefore, stresses the militant aspect of the Kingdom. Origen, on the other hand, emphasizes especially the blissful presence of God in the human soul, while Cyril of Jerusalem fixes his attention on the eschatological conception. He closely unites the Kingdom of Heaven with the Last Judgement and its consequences for the just, so that it is practically identified with beatitude.

The contrast with Origen, under the influence of whose school Gregory had been nurtured, is most noticeable in his exegesis of the fourth petition. For Origen it goes without saying that the daily bread of the Our Father is no ordinary bread; Jesus said we ought to ask for great and heavenly things, and material bread could not be counted among such (27.1). He then proves from Scripture that there we can find the term "bread" used in many senses. Our Lord means by it sometimes faith, sometimes Himself, but above all His Eucharistic Body. Consequently he interprets the term ἐπιούσιος as substantial, deriving it from οὐσία. Thus the bread in the Lord's Prayer becomes the substantial bread that nourishes our souls and gives them health, strength, and, finally, immortality. For Gregory, on the other hand, it is the ordinary material bread, and, more generally, everything necessary for the preservation of our physical existence, excluding luxuries. He also contradicts Origen in stressing that we not only may, but ought to, pray for earthly things. Hence he cannot but abandon Origen's derivation of ἐπιούσιος from οὐσία and renders it simply as "daily." Moreover, he refers or limits the "today" of the petition to the individual day, and concludes that we should not take care for the morrow. Origen, on the contrary, illustrates by many Scriptural arguments that in Biblical usage "daily" is frequently understood of the whole present dispensation, and so understands it in the Lord's Prayer. He even takes the opportunity to discuss the various periods of the world which Scripture symbolizes by days. Cyril of Jerusalem is even more explicit in his Eucharistic interpretation of the passage, and follows Origen's rendering of ἐπιούσιος. Both Origen and Cyril reject the literal exegesis of "bread." In this, then, Gregory's interpretation is original.

He further differs from his predecessors by introducing Original Sin into his interpretation of the fifth and sixth petitions. Cyril does not mention it at all, and Origen has only a few allusions, though he places great emphasis on the doctrine in other contexts, for instance, in *Contra Celsum* 3.62 and 66. According to Gregory, when we recite the fifth petition of the Our Father, we daily confess that we still commit sins. These sins are twofold. On the one hand, we all have our share in the guilt of Adam, inherent in our nature by the very fact that we are human. This alone should prevent a man from thinking himself to be without sin. On the other hand, our conscience testifies that we commit many actual sins throughout our life. Indeed, we need but look at the dangers surrounding us on all sides to see how difficult and really impossible it is not to fall into sin. No one, Gregory asserts, can boast of being without sin; hence no one can dispense himself from the fifth petition.

Gregory stresses especially the interrelation between Divine and human forgiveness. If we would be forgiven, we must ourselves forgive. If we would approach God with the petition for pardon, we must first become like Him, especially by ridding ourselves of all harshness and cruelty towards our neighbour. For it would contradict the most elementary conceptions of justice if we received forgiveness without granting it ourselves. Gregory makes effective use of antithesis when inculcating this truth, and, like Origen, he adduces the parable of the unjust steward. But he leaves both Origen and Cyril far behind in emphasizing the idea of retribution. The reader can scarcely resist the impression that God forgives our sins because he is forced to do so by our own forgiveness, whereas He pardons freely from His great love and mercy. Origen and Cyril had not gone thus far. With them, too, God appears as partner in an agreement, but they do not lose sight of the fact that in the last resort we owe everything to God's goodness. They, too, stress that a good deed deserves a recompense. But Gregory goes further and alleges that our forgiveness is actually an example which God is bound to imitate. It is true, he apologizes for this audacity; yet he maintains that God could not possibly suffer Himself to be surpassed by our human generosity. God is bound to imitate man's good example and forgive in His turn. Even though the sins which God has to forgive are greater than those of our debtors, this disparity is made up by God's infinitely superior power and perfection.

For Gregory as for Origen and Cyril the forgiveness of sins and charity towards one's neighbour are the aim of the fifth petition. But Gregory does not rest satisfied with this. He adds a new idea by bringing in the deification of man. Since God alone has the right to forgive sins, by imitating Him in this man in some way becomes like unto God and his nature is divinized. Having thus reached the summit of virtue, man ascends even above the perfection of the angels.

In his exegesis of the sixth petition Gregory interprets "temptation" in a way Origen and Cyril had rejected. Origen thought a literal interpretation impossible because, in his view, our whole life is made up of temptations which are, indeed, the necessary consequence of our bodily nature. Hence he cannot admit that temptations should cease, but explains the petition as a prayer to be preserved from succumbing to them. Cyril goes a step further. Whereas Origen saw temptation as an occasional yielding to the charms of sin, Cyril has in view the final defeat by sin, from which there is no recovery. Therefore we pray here to be preserved from an irrevocable fall. Gregory, on the other hand, takes the temptations to be attacks of the Evil One, who tries to gain our soul by the bait of the allurements of the world. Hence, when the soul is withdrawn from the world—not when it has rid itself from concupiscence—temptation has no possibility of approaching it. Here Gregory's inclination towards the asceticism of the desert shows itself unmistakably. According to him we actually save ourselves from evil by escaping from the world, just as one can save oneself by flight from being drowned in the sea, burned by fire, or killed in war. In the world, of course, temptations are inevitable, since the world lies in the Evil One; they cease, however, if we escape from the world. This idea of the world as a bait and the possibility of avoiding its temptations is typical of Gregory. It enables him to explain God's share in temptation in some ways more satisfactorily than Origen and Cyril. For Origen's conception poses the question how God can lead us into defeat in our struggle with sin. Origen, indeed, tries to meet it by conceiving temptation as a transitory state leading to purification. But besides being somewhat far-fetched this reply does not really solve the difficulty. Cyril's interpretation of temptation as final apostasy is even more untenable, since it really would exclude God's share in it altogether. Yet Gregory's exegesis is equally defective. On the one hand, he attributes the escape to man's own initiative in fleeing from the world rather than to God; on the other hand, escape from the world does not really protect against temptation, as the case of St. Anthony and so many other desert Fathers so clearly shows.

We see, then, that Gregory follows the traditional teaching, but without giving up his independence. His "Origenism" is often no more than an agreement in form, which he then proceeds to fill with his own personal contents.

In the sermons on the Beatitudes the teaching given is on a somewhat higher level, as befits its subject. The Beatitudes, as has been said before, are represented under the image of a ladder, by means of which the Divine Word leads us from one step to the other, up to the heights of martyrdom. Here again the very elevated teaching on Christian perfection is enlivened by vivid descriptions of the life of the times, of the follies and sufferings of men. The exegesis deals usually first with the literal sense of the Beatitude under consideration, and then goes on to bring out a more sublime meaning.

Gregory of Nyssa is one of the great mystic theologians of antiquity. Throughout his life he was occupied with the question of the vision and knowledge of God. As the Beatific Vision is the highest object of life in Heaven, we ought even here on earth to strive to know God as far as possible. He takes it for granted that we can know God by our natural reason and that we can prove His existence from the order of the cosmos and the perfection of creatures. But he desires more than this elementary knowledge, which is also accessible to pagan philosophy.

The vision of God in the mirror of the pure soul can be attained only by Christians, who reach it through their cooperation with grace.[10]   If man's life is pure, the original image, in which he was created and which was darkened by sin, will shine forth in new splendour.   By contemplating this image in ourselves we can form a conception of the Divine perfections.   This is one of Gregory's favourite subjects, which he has expounded nowhere with greater clarity than in his sixth sermon on the Beatitudes.   He never applies the vision of God promised to the clean of heart to the Beatific Vision in the next world.   Yet St. John the Evangelist, St. Paul, and even Moses, teach unequivocally that no man has ever seen God in this life. Hence the Beatitude cannot mean that we shall be able to see God's essence already here on earth.   On the other hand, it is impossible that the vision of God promised by Christ should be the same knowledge that is also accessible to the non-Christian philosophers.   Thus there must be an intermediary knowledge between the vision of His essence and the natural knowledge through creatures.

Gregory illustrates his meaning by a parallel.   It is of little avail to know health only by hearsay; one must know it because one possesses it.   In the same way the Beatitude of which Our Lord speaks consists less in knowing something about God, but in possessing Him within oneself. Indeed, as Gregory points out, Scripture frequently uses the term "see" in the sense of "possessing."   The Christian must realize in himself the word of Christ: "The Kingdom of God is within you."   The soul of man is created in the image of God as a mirror reflecting Him.[11]   But like a metal mirror defaced by rust, the soul stained by sin no longer shows this image.   The rust must be removed from the mirror, which is the soul, so that its original beauty may reappear.   We achieve this by developing the virtues of the soul, especially purity and freedom from passions, which latter conception he treats with wise moderation, especially in the second and sixth sermons. These virtues which lead us to sanctity establish in us the Kingdom of God and restore the Image. Just as one sees the sun itself when one sees it reflected in a mirror, so also the man who is purified from passion sees God Himself when he perceives His image in his soul. But this metaphor of the mirrored image of God must not mislead us. If such a man "sees himself, he sees in himself what he desires." [12] In the act of mystic contemplation man immediately apprehends the perfectly pure in the reflexion of his own image, and so he does not need the discursive reasoning of ordinary knowledge.

Hence the promise of seeing God is realized in the intimate union with Him, which is the fruit of a pure life. The Gospel teaches us how to achieve this purity by keeping the Commandments and practising asceticism. The ideal of the Christian life is expressed in the words of the Canticle: *My Beloved to me and I to Him.* This means being empty of all but God, and, by fixing one's regard only on the immaterial and spiritual, to become a pure image of the Divine Beauty. The same ideal is expressed in the words of St. Paul: *Christ is my life.* This, too, means detachment from all that might stain the soul, so that it may be filled with God who is purity, immortality, light, and truth. [13]

This teaching is certainly thoroughly Christian. Yet whoever knows the *Enneads* of Plotinus will realize how close is the connection between the conceptions of Gregory and Neo-Platonist philosophy. [14] The Neoplatonists, too, teach that purification leads to deification, and that the former consists in removing the passions and acquiring virtue. The beauty of the soul lies in her likeness to the Divine, in which God's beauty is reflected. It is Gregory's achievement that he has Christianized his Neo-Platonist borrowings so that but little remains that is foreign to Christian spirituality.

There is, nevertheless, one feature in both the treatises, which may perhaps shock the modern reader. It is the seeming assumption that it is entirely in the power of man to reach the goal of perfection. Gregory argues repeatedly that the mercy God will show to man is entirely dependent on the mercy man shows to his fellows; there is no mention of grace, which first enables man to show mercy at all. This is, indeed, a defect of almost all Greek theology. But in reading these Fathers we have always to remember that neither Augustine nor Pelagius had argued this subject when they wrote, and that, generally, the question of grace never arose in the East, because no particular heresy on this matter had been propounded there. Moreover, it is undeniable that Greek ascetical teaching was greatly indebted to Stoic philosophy, and that the emphasis on human effort learned in this school was not always fully balanced by the corresponding stress on Divine grace that should have been learned from St. Paul. On the other hand, the two treatises presented here were series of sermons meant to spur the hearers to greater effort, hence the predominance of the human factor is all the more understandable.

The picture of Gregory of Nyssa that emerges from the two works here presented should be attractive to the modern reader. It is that of a man thoroughly conversant with human nature in general and the needs of his contemporaries in particular; not a Desert Father, living in isolation from the world around him—a world that presents many features similar to our own—but steeped in its culture and interested in all it has to offer. At the same time, the former rhetor has found that, attractive though this world may often be, the only goal worth living for is the Kingdom of Heaven; and having become a bishop and shepherd of souls, he uses all his powers and knowledge to imbue others with the same conviction.

As we have said in the beginning, it is unfortunate that there should be no modern critical editions of these treatises. I have followed for *The Lord's Prayer* the best old edition, that of Krabinger, 1840, and for *The Beatitudes* the Paris edition of 1638, reproduced by Migne, *Patrologia Graeca* 44.1193–1302.

The Latin translation by Sifanus is reproduced by Migne; Krabinger has his own Latin translation for his edition of *The Lord's Prayer*. A German translation of the same work appeared in *Bibliothek der Kirchenväter*, 2. ed., vol. 56, by K. Weiss (Munich 1927).

THE LORD'S PRAYER

SERMON 1

The Divine Word teaches us the science of prayer. And to the disciples worthy of it, who eagerly asked to learn to pray in such a way as to win the favour of the Divine hearing, this science is proposed in the words that prayer should take. Now, I make bold to add a little to what Scripture says; for the present congregation needs instruction not so much on how to pray, as on the necessity of praying at all, a necessity that has perhaps not yet been grasped by most people. In fact, the majority of men grievously neglect in their life this sacred and divine work which is prayer. In this matter, therefore, I think it right first of all to insist as much as possible that one must persevere in prayer, as the Apostle says; [1] secondly, that we must listen attentively to the Divine Voice which proposes to us the manner in which we should offer prayer to the Lord. For I see that in this present life men give their attention to everything else, one concentrating on this matter, another on that; but no one devotes his zeal to the good work of prayer.

The tradesman rises early to attend to his shop, anxious to display his wares sooner than his competitors so as to get in before them, to be the first to attend to the customer and sell his stock. The customer does the same; he takes good care not to miss what he wants by letting someone else anticipate him; and so he hastens not to church but to the market. Thus all are equally keen on gain and anxious to be on the spot before their neighbours, and the hour for prayer is usurped by those things that hold their interest and is turned into time for trafficking.

It is the same with the craftsman, with the orator, with the man who brings a lawsuit as well as with the judge; everyone devotes all his energy to the work he has in hand, forgetting completely the work of prayer because he thinks that the time he gives to God is lost to the work he has purposed to do. For the craftsman considers that the Divine assistance is quite useless for the work he has in hand. Therefore he leaves prayer aside and places all his hopes in his hands, without remembering Him who has given him his hands. In the same way someone who carefully composes a speech does not think of Him who has given him speech; but he pursues his own and his pupils' studies as if he had brought himself into this existence; hence he fails to realize that something good might come to him through the action of God and prefers study to prayer. It is the same with the other occupations: the fact that the mind centres its attention on material, earthly things prevents the soul from devoting itself to the better, heavenly things. Thus it comes about that life is so full of sin, which is always increasing in growth and involved in all human pursuits; therefore everyone keeps forgetting God, and men do not count prayer among the good things worth pursuing. Covetousness enters together with trade; but covetousness is idolatry.[2]

Thus the husbandman does not cultivate the land according to his needs, but is always intent on getting more, and so makes a large entrance for sin in his profession by enlarging his property at the expense of others. Hence

arise disputes which are difficult to compose, people becoming incensed against each other over their boundaries,
because they are all afflicted with the same disease of
covetousness. Hence arise feuds, occasions of evil and attacks on one another that often end in bloodshed and
murder. In the same way the contentions in the courts
give rise to a variety of sins and find a host of excuses for
injustice. The judge, for example, may either wilfully
incline the balance of justice towards the side of gain, or
be involuntarily misled by the subtlety of those who dis-
tort the truth, and thus gives an unjust judgement. But
how could anyone describe in detail all the different ways
in which sin is mixed up with human life? And the reason
for this is none other than that men will not ask the help
of God for the things they have in hand.

If work is preceded by prayer, sin will find no entrance
into the soul. For when the consciousness of God is
firmly established in the heart, the devices of the devil
remain sterile, and matters of dispute will always be settled
according to justice. Prayer prevents the farmer from
committing sin, for his fruit will multiply even on a small
plot of land, so that sin no longer enters together with the
desire for more. It is the same with everyone; with the
traveller, with somebody who prepares an expedition or a
marriage. Whatever anyone may set out to do, if it is
done with prayer the undertaking will prosper and he will
be kept from sin, because there is nothing to oppose him
and drag the soul into passion.[3] If, on the other hand, a
man leaves God out and gives his attention to nothing but
his business, then he is inevitably opposed to God, because
he is separated from Him. For a person who does not
unite himself to God through prayer is separated from God.

Therefore we must learn first of all *that we ought always to pray and not to faint*.[4] For the effect of prayer is union with God, and if someone is with God, he is separated from the enemy. Through prayer we guard our chastity, control our temper, and rid ourselves of vanity; it makes us forget injuries, overcomes envy, defeats injustice, and makes amends for sin. Through prayer we obtain physical well-being, a happy home, and a strong, well-ordered society. Prayer will make our nation powerful, will give us victory in war and security in peace; it reconciles enemies and preserves allies. Prayer is the seal of virginity and a pledge of faithfulness in marriage; it shields the wayfarer, protects the sleeper, and gives courage to those who keep vigil. It obtains a good harvest for the farmer and a safe port for the sailor.

Prayer is your advocate in lawsuits. If you are in prison, it will obtain your release; it will refresh you when you are weary and comfort you when you are sorrowful. Prayer is the delight of the joyful as well as solace to the afflicted. It is the wedding crown [5] of the spouses and the festive joy of a birthday no less than the shroud that enwraps us in death.

Prayer is intimacy with God and contemplation of the invisible. It satisfies our yearnings and makes us equal to the angels. Through it good prospers, evil is destroyed, and sinners will be converted. Prayer is the enjoyment of things present and the substance of the things to come. Prayer turned the whale into a home for Jonas; it brought Ezechias back to life from the very gates of death; it transformed the flames into a moist wind for the Three Children. Through prayer the Israelites triumphed over the Amalecites, and 185,000 Assyrians were slain in one night

by the invisible sword.[6] Past history furnishes thousands
of other examples beside these which make it clear that of
all the things valued in this life nothing is more precious
than prayer. I wish we could already turn to prayer itself;
but we would rather add a little to what has been said, and
consider how many diverse good things we have received
from Divine grace, for the gift of which we should make
a return to our Benefactor by prayer and thanksgiving.

Now I think that, even if we spent our whole life in
constant communion with God in prayer and thanksgiving, we should be as far from having made Him an adequate return as if we had not even begun to desire making
the Giver of all good things such a return.

Time is measured by a threefold division, past, present,
and future. In all three we receive the munificence of the
Lord. If you consider the present, it is through Him that
you live; if the future, your hope that your expectations
might be fulfilled is founded on Him; if the past, you will
realize that you did not even exist before He made you.
Your very birth you have received as a benefit from Him;
and once born, another benefit was conferred on you in
that, as the Apostle says, you should live and move in
Him.[7] The hopes of the future depend upon the same
Divine action. You, however, are master only of the present. Therefore, even if you never cease to give thanks to
God throughout your life, you will hardly thank Him for
the present; and as for the future and the past, you will not
be able to find a means of rendering Him His due.

Yet, though we are so far from being able to thank Him
properly, we do not even show our good intention as far
as we can—I will not say all day long, but not even by devoting a tiny part of the day to the service of God. Who

has spread the earth under my feet? Whose wisdom has made water passable? Who has set up the vault of the sky? Who carries the sun before me like a torch? Who causes the springs to come forth from ravines? Who has given the rivers their beds? Who has subjected the animals to my service? Who, when I was but lifeless ashes, gave me both life and a mind? Who fashioned this clay in the image of the Divine? [8] And, when this Divine Image had been tarnished by sin, did not He restore it to its former beauty? When I was exiled from Paradise, deprived of the tree of life, and submerged in the gulf of material things, was it not He who brought me back to man's first beatitude? *There is none that understandeth*, says the Scripture. [9]

Truly, if we considered these things, we should give thanks all our life without ceasing; but actually human nature is almost completely involved in the pursuit of material things. For these it is eagerly ready, with these memory and hope are occupied. In its desire for more, human nature gives itself no rest whatever where there is a chance of gain. Whether it be a question of honour and reputation, of abundant wealth, or of the disease of carnal appetite, in all these things nature desires increase. Yet to the truly good things of God, both those that can already be seen and those that are promised, no thought is given. But it is time to consider as far as we are able the meaning of the words of the prayer.

It is clear that in order to obtain our desires we must learn how we ought to pray. What, then, are we taught about it? *When you are praying, do not babble as the heathens. For they think that in their much speaking they may be heard.* [10] Perhaps the meaning of the teaching is quite clear in itself. It is cast in rather simple language. It needs no subtle learning, except that it is worth discussing what is meant by the term *battalogia* (babbling), so that by realizing its sense we may avoid what is forbidden. It seems to me that He is castigating empty minds and crushing those who immerse themselves in vain desires. Hence He invented this strange novelty of a word in order to rebuke those foolish people who rush hither and thither in order to gratify their desires for completely useless things. For the sensible and rational word, which is concerned with useful things, is properly called a *logos* (word), but that which is poured forth by vain desires for empty pleasures is not a *logos*, but a *battalogia*. And if anyone would explain the meaning in better Greek, he would say *phlyaria* (nonsense) or *leros* (humbug) or *phlenaphos* (chatter), or something like that.

Which advice, therefore, does this passage give us? That in the time of prayer we should not allow such things to enter as passion puts into the mind of fools. For example, childish people do not reflect how a thing could possibly take place according to their fancy, but they imagine for all they are worth wonderful things happening to themselves. They daydream about riches, marriages and kingdoms and big cities that are to be called by their name, and they imagine that they actually are in such a position as their silly ideas suggest.

There are people who are gripped even more violently by this folly. Passing beyond the limits of nature, they develop wings or shine like stars, or carry mountains in their hands; they journey through the heavens or live for myriads of years, becoming young again in their old age, and whatever other bubbles the empty mind of childish people may throw up. Now supposing someone was engaged in some work and did not give his attention to things promising good results, but busied himself with ridiculous aspirations—he would be making a pitiful fool of himself, wasting on these daydreams the time he ought to spend thinking out some profitable proposition. In the same way if a man during prayer is not intent on what profits his soul, but would rather that God should fall in with the emotional [11] uncertainties of his own mind, he is truly like a silly *battalogos*, who prays that God should become a willing servant of his own crazy ideas.

To give an example. Someone approaches God in prayer, but failing to appreciate the exalted greatness whom he is addressing, unwittingly insulted His majesty with nothing but base petitions. It is just as if a very poor and uneducated man who thought earthenware precious, approached a king who had decided to distribute riches and honours. But the poor man would not make requests worthy of the king, but ask from so great a personage to take clay and make it into something according to his own mind. In the same way the man who makes prayer without being properly taught, will not lift himself up to the height of the Giver, but wants the Divine power to descend to the mean, earthly level of his own desires. Therefore he offers unruly cravings to Him who sees into the hearts, not desiring Him to heal the perverse movements of his mind, but to make them worse, for through the help of God the evil desire would become a fact. Because someone gives me pain and my heart hates him it says to God: Strike him; almost crying out: Let my own passion be in Thee, and may my wickedness pass over into Thee. Obviously, just as in human fights one cannot support one of the parties without sharing in the anger of the person who is infuriated against his opponent, thus it is also clear that he who tries to set God against his enemy, asks Him to share his own angry excitement. But this means that the Divine should succumb to passion, behave in a human manner and change from His own natural goodness into the ferocity of a beast.

Such is the behaviour of a man mad after fame, or of one who in his arrogance lusts for more; these are the manners of men bent on winning a lawsuit, pressing for the crown in the games or ambitious for fame in the theatre, often also of those consumed with the insane passions of youth. They all do not pray to God that they might be delivered from the disease that holds them captive, but that the disease might be brought to perfection. And if they fail to obtain these things, each one holds this to be a calamity. Truly they babble nonsense, imploring God to become their fellow patient in this mental disease. Worst of all, they want to move the Divine towards contrary desires, they would divide the power of God into two, namely into savagery and lovingkindness. On the one hand they want Him to be gracious and gentle to themselves, on the other they ask Him to show Himself hard and bitter to their enemies. Oh, the folly of the babblers! For if God is harsh to them, He will not be mild to you. If you hope that He will be inclined to show mercy to you, how can He change to the opposite, from mercy to bitterness?

But argumentative people anticipate such reproach and immediately adduce words from prophecy in defence of their own bitterness, such as those of David who desires sinners to faint away and calls down shame and confusion on his enemies; [12] or of Jeremias who desires to see God revenge him on his enemies, [13] and Osee asking that his adversaries may be given a childless womb and dry breasts. [14] And they collect many sayings which are scattered throughout the Holy Scriptures and prove from them that one should pray against one's enemies; and thus they want God's kindness to co-operate with their own bitterness. But in order to stop the babblers who have been led from such starting-point to its opposite, we shall deal with this objection point by point.

Of the true Saints, inspired by the Holy Spirit, whose sayings have been recorded by Divine dispensation for the instruction of later generations, none can be shown to have desired anything evil; but their words aim solely at the correction of the evil that is holding sway over human nature. Thus, in the same way as a man who prays that there may be no sick or no poor, does not want that such people should be exterminated, but that sickness and want should cease, so every Saint, too, must be understood if he prays for the destruction of what is utterly hostile to nature; though this may put into the heads of the ill-instructed the idea that he is greatly incensed against men.

If the Psalmist says, *Let sinners be consumed out of the earth and the unjust, so that they be no more,* [15] he prays that sin and injustice may be destroyed. For man is not man's enemy, but the evil movement of free will ranges within the order of enemies what is united by nature. If he prays, therefore, that evil may cease, this does not mean that man is something evil; for how could the image of good be evil? [16] Hence when he calls down shame and confusion on his enemies he shows you the battle array of adversaries coming forth from the invisible fiend to fight against the life of man. About these St. Paul speaks plainly in greater detail when he says that *our wrestling is against principalities, against powers and the rulers of this world, against the spirits of wickedness in the high places.*[17] There are the diabolic plots by which wicked opportunities of sin are devised for men, occasions for wrath, inducements to lust, matter for envy, hate, pride, and similar evils. When the great prophet prays against the enemies, he asks that such things may be put to shame which he sees treacherously agitating the soul of everyone.

Now this means that the enemy may be saved, for it is natural that someone who has been defeated in a fight should be ashamed of his defeat, just as contrariwise the victor glories in his victory. That this is so is made clear by the form of the prayer. For he says: *Let them be confounded and ashamed that seek after my soul.*[18] For he does not utter imprecations against those who make plots for financial damage, or who dispute about the boundaries of land, or plan bodily harm against him, but against those who design evil against his soul. But what is an evil design against the soul if not estrangement from God? Now the human soul cannot be alienated from God except through a mind enslaved by passions. For as the Divine Nature is altogether impassible,[19] a man who is always entangled in passions is debarred from union with God. In order not to suffer this the Psalmist prays for the confusion of his enemies. This is what is meant by praying for his own victory against his enemies; for these enemies are the passions. Jeremias in his zeal for God's worship did the same: when the king and his subjects with him were mad on idols, he did not trouble about his own suffering, but prayed for the common good of men that through the attack against the godless all men might be brought to their senses.

So also the prophet, seeing how widespread evil was among the Israelites of the time, rightly condemns the people to childlessness and desires the bitter breasts of sin to dry up, so that evil may not be born and bred among men. Therefore he says, *Give them, O Lord, a womb without children and dry breasts.* And whatever other expressions signifying indictment and wrath be found in the Saints bear a similar meaning, that is to say, they want not to destroy man but to abolish evil.[20] *God made not death.* Do you hear the denial? How then should he be likely to ask God for the death of his enemies, seeing that God is a stranger to death? He does not delight in the perdition of the living. But he who babbles and wants to rouse the Divine lovingkindness against his personal enemies, asks Him to delight in human misery.

But, it might be said, some people who desired offices, honours, and riches, and obtained them by having recourse to prayer, were believed to be loved by God on account of their good fortune. Why then would you prevent us from asking God for such things?

Now it is quite obvious, and nobody would deny it, that all things depend indeed on the Divine Will, and that life here below is ordered from above. But we have learned that there are other causes for the success of such prayers. Not as if God did not dispense to those that ask Him also these things as something good; but this is done in order that through it the faith of the weak should be confirmed. They will gradually learn from their experience with smaller petitions that God hears their supplications, so that they may rise to the desire for the higher gifts which are more worthy of God. It is the same as we see in our children. For a time they cling to their mother's breast, sucking from it as much as nature can hold; but when the baby grows up and becomes capable of speech, he despises the breast and seeks other things, whether the pinned-on front locks [21] or the mantle or some such things that delight the eyes of infants. But when he grows still older and his mind develops with his body, he leaves behind all childish desires and asks his parents for those things that belong to the adult life.

It is the same in relation to God, who often is not deaf even to man's smallest petitions in order to accustom him to look to Him for everything; for so He can call a man who has obtained this gracious favour in small things to the desire for the higher ones. And if somebody or other has by Divine Providence become famous and admired despite his humble origin, or has obtained anything else of the things that are sought after in this life, such as high office or riches or publicity, you must consider the purpose of these things. This is that the love of God manifested in them should show forth His power, so that, because you have obtained these childish toys, you might offer the Father petitions for the greater and more perfect things. For those are the things that profit the soul.

It would be a very silly thing, indeed, to approach God in order to seek temporal things from the Eternal, earthly goods from Heavenly Goodness. For this means to seek low things from the Highest, some contemptible temporal good fortune from Him who bestows the Kingdom of Heaven; to seek from Him who gives those things that cannot be taken away the temporary use of some inessential trifles which will certainly be taken away, which are enjoyed only for a little time, and the use of which is fraught with danger. Well does He show the absurdity of such requests by adding *as the heathens.* For to be eagerly interested in the things of sense is characteristic of those who have neither hope in the world to come nor fear of judgement and the threat of hell. Since they expect none of the good things for which we hope in the resurrection, they are, like cattle, concerned only with the present life, how to indulge their palate and stomach and the desire for other luxuries of the body. They consider desirable either to be esteemed quite superior to the rest of men or to sit on many moneybags, or whatever else may belong to the deceits of this life. But if anyone speaks to them of the hope to come he seems to them a perfect fool, raving about Paradise and the life of the Kingdom of Heaven and so on. Since then attachment to the present life is the characteristic of those who are without hope, Scripture rightly says that the quite superfluous desires which people addicted to pleasure fancy to get fulfilled by prayer belong to the heathens. For they suppose that if they persist in asking for these absurdities, the Divinity will help to get them however unfitting they may be. *For* they think, He says, *that in their much speaking they may be heard.* Now through what we have just been considering we have learned what we ought to know. But what kind of prayer we ought to offer to God we will consider next time, by the grace of Our Lord Jesus Christ to whom be glory and power for ever and ever. Amen.

SERMON 2

Our Father, who art in Heaven.

When the great Moses undertook to initiate the Israelites into the Divine mysteries [22] which had been inaugurated on the Mount,[23] he did not deem them ready to receive the theophany until he had ordained the purification of the people by chastity and the sprinkling of water. But even so they did not brave the manifestation of the Divine power, but were struck down by all the apparitions, the fire and the darkness, the smoke and the trumpets. So they turned back and asked the Lawgiver to be their mediator of the will of God, seeing that they were not fit by their own power to draw near to God to receive the Divine manifestation.

But when our Lawgiver the Lord Jesus Christ is bringing us to Divine grace, He does not present Mount Sinai covered with darkness and smoking with fire,[24] nor does He strike fear into us by the meaningless sound of trumpets. He does not purify the soul by three days' chastity and by water that washes dirt away; nor does He leave all the assembly behind at the foot of the mountain, granting only to one the ascent to its summit, which, moreover, is hidden by a darkness completely concealing the glory of God. But, first of all, He leads us not to a mountain but to Heaven itself, which He has rendered accessible to men by virtue. Secondly, He gives them not only the vision of, but a share in, the Divine power, bringing them as it were to kinship with the Divine Nature. Moreover, He

35

does not hide the supernal glory in darkness, making it difficult for those who want to contemplate it; but He first illumines the darkness by the brilliant light of His teaching and then grants the pure of heart the vision of the ineffable glory in shining splendour. The water He gives us for sprinkling does not come from alien streams, but wells up in ourselves, whether we understand by it the fountains of tears streaming from our eyes, or the pure conscience of the heart that admits no impurity coming from evil; He proclaims as a law chastity not only from the lawful intercourse between husband and wife, but that springing from a nature entangled in material passions, and thus leads us to God through prayer. For this is the force of His words, that we should learn by them not to pronounce certain sounds and syllables, but the meaning of the ascent to God which is accomplished through a sublime way of life.

But now it is time that we should learn the Divine discipline through the words of the prayer itself. *When you pray*, He says. He does not say "When you make a vow," [25] but "When you pray": a vowed promise ought to have been made before approaching God in prayer. Now what is the difference in meaning between these words? It is this: a vow (*euche*) is the promise of something consecrated to the service of God; whereas prayer (*proseuche*) is the offering to God of a supplication for good things. Since, therefore, we need confidence [26] to approach God with the request for the things that are profitable for us, the performance of a vow must necessarily come first. Thus, when we have accomplished our part, we are confident of being made worthy to receive in return the things that are God's to give.

Therefore says the Prophet, *I will pay Thee my vows, which my lips have uttered,*[27] and *Vow ye and pay to the Lord your God.*[28] And this meaning of *euche* can be seen in many places in Scripture, so that we should know, as has been said, that *euche* is the promise of a thank offering; whereas *proseuche* signifies our approaching God after the fulfilment of the promise. Hence the passage teaches us not to ask something from God without first having offered Him an acceptable gift. One must first vow (*euxasthai*) and then pray (*proseuxasthai*); first the sowing, then the fruitbearing, so to speak. Hence we must first cast the seed of the vow, and thus reap what has grown from this sowing, receiving grace in return for prayer. Since, then, there can be no confidence in relationship with God unless we have prepared our approach to Him by vow and the offering of gifts, *euche* must precede *proseuche.*

Assuming therefore that this has already been done, the Lord says to His disciples: *When you pray, say: Our Father, who art in Heaven.*[29] *Who will give me wings like a dove*, says the great David somewhere in the Psalms.[30] This I, too, would say, boldly using the same words. Who will give me those wings, that my mind may wing its way up to the heights of these noble words? Then I would leave behind the earth altogether and traverse all the middle air; I would reach the beautiful ether, come to the stars and behold all their orderly array.[31] But not even there would I stop short, but, passing beyond them, would become a stranger to all that moves and changes, and apprehend the stable Nature, the immovable Power which exists in its own right, guiding and keeping in being all things, for all depend on the ineffable will of the Divine Wisdom.

So first my mind must become detached from anything subject to flux and change and tranquilly rest in motionless spiritual repose, so as to be rendered akin to Him who is perfectly unchangeable; and then it may address Him by this most familiar name and say: Father.

What spirit a man must have to say this word—what confidence, what purity of conscience! Supposing a man should try to understand God as far as possible from the names that have been invented for Him and so be led to the understanding of the ineffable glory: he would have learned that the Divine Nature, whatever It may be in Itself, is absolute goodness, holiness and joy, power, glory and purity, eternity that is always absolutely the same. These and whatever other things thought could learn about the Divine Nature, whether from the Divine Scriptures or from its own meditation, he would consider—and after all that should he dare to utter such a word and call this Being his Father? If he has any sense, he would obviously not dare to call God by the name Father since he does not see the same things in himself as he sees in God. For it is physically impossible that He who is good by essence should be the Father of an evil will, nor the Holy One of him whose life is impure. No more can He who is changeless be the Father of a man who is turning from one side to the other, nor can the Father of life have as His son someone whom sin has subjected to death. He who is wholly pure cannot be the Father of those who have disgraced themselves by unseemly passions, nor He who pours out benefits of him who is self-seeking. In short, He who is seen to be pure goodness cannot be Father of those who are wholly involved in some evil. If therefore on examining himself a man finds that he still needs to be purified because his conscience is full of vile stains and sores, he cannot insinuate himself into the family of God until he has been purged from all these evil things. The unjust and impure cannot say Father to the just and pure, since this would mean calling God Father of his own wickedness, which would be nothing but pride and mockery. For the word Father indicates the cause of what exists through Him.

Hence if a man whose conscience accuses him of evil calls God his Father, he asserts precisely that God is the cause and origin of his own wickedness. But *there is no fellowship of light with darkness,* says the Apostle; [32] but light associates with light and justice with what is just, beauty with what is beautiful and incorruption with the incorruptible. *A good tree cannot bring forth evil fruit.*[33] If then someone who is *dull of heart* and *seeks after lying,*[34] as the Scripture says, yet dares to use the words of the prayer, he should know that he does not call the Heavenly One his Father, but the infernal one, who is himself a liar and father of every lie, who is sin and the father of sin.[35] Hence the Apostle calls men who are subject to the passions *children of wrath,*[36] and one who has fallen away from the true life is named *the son of perdition;*[37] someone who is lazy and effeminate is termed *the son of deserting maidens.*[38] In the same way, conversely, those whose conscience is pure are called *children of light and day,*[39] and others who aspire to the Divine strength sons of power.[40]

If therefore the Lord teaches us in His prayer to call God Father, it seems to me that He is doing nothing else but to set the most sublime life before us as our law. For Truth does not teach us to deceive, to say we are what we are not and to use a name to which we have no right. But if we call our Father Him who is incorruptible and just and good, we must prove by our life that the kinship is real. Do you see how much preparation we need, and what kind of life we must lead? How ardent must be our zeal so that our conscience may achieve such purity as to have the courage to say "Father" to God? For if you make such prayer with your lips while you are keen on money and occupied with the deceits of the world, while you are seeking fame among men or are enslaved by sensual passions—what, do you think, will He say to it who sees your life and knows what your prayer really is? It seems to me that God would say to such a man something like this: You, whose life is corrupt, call the Author of incorruption Father? Why do you defile the pure name with your polluted word? Why do you belie this word and insult the undefiled Nature? If you were my child, your life would be marked by my own good qualities. I do not recognize the image of my Nature in you. Your characteristics are the exact opposite of mine. *What fellowship hath light with darkness?* [41] What kinship has death with life? How can there be intimacy between pure and impure? The Giver of good things is far removed from the man who is covetous. There can be no intercourse between Him who is merciful and him who is cruel. The evils that are in you have another for their father; for my offspring are made lovely by the goodness of their Father. The child of the Merciful and Pure is himself merciful and pure; the corrupt is not related to the incorrupt. In a word, good comes from good and just from just. But as to you, I know not whence you are. Therefore it is dangerous to dare to use this prayer and call God one's Father before one's life has been purified.

But let us once more listen to the words of the prayer, if perhaps, through frequent repetition, we may be given to understand some of its hidden meaning. *Our Father, who art in Heaven.* That one must win God's favour by a virtuous life has been made sufficiently clear through what has been said before. But the words seem to me to indicate a deeper meaning, for they remind us of the fatherland from which we have fallen and of the noble birthright which we have lost. Thus in the story of the young man who left his father's home and went away to live after the manner of swine the Word shows the misery of men in the form of a parable which tells of his departure and dissolute life; and He does not bring him back to his former happiness until he has become sensibly aware of his present plight and entered into himself, rehearsing words of repentance. Now these words agree as it were with the words of the prayer, for he said, *Father, I have sinned against Heaven and before thee.*[42] He would not have added to his confession the sin against Heaven, if he had not been convinced that the country he had left when he sinned was Heaven. Therefore this confession gave him easy access to the father who ran towards him and embraced and kissed him. And this signifies the yoke of the Word, which had been placed on man through the mouth, that is to say, through the tradition of the Gospel, after he had thrown off the first yoke of the commandment by shaking himself free of the protecting law. And he put on him the robe, not another one, but the first robe, of which he had been deprived by his disobedience,[43] when he had tasted of the forbidden fruit and seen his own nakedness. The ring on his hand, because of the carved stone, signifies the regaining of the Image. But he also protects his feet with shoes so that if he approaches the head of the serpent, it may not bite into his naked heel. Thus the return of the young man to his Father's home became to him the occasion of experiencing the lovingkindness of his Father; for this paternal home is the Heaven against which, as he says to his Father, he has sinned. In the same way it seems to me that if the Lord is teaching us to call upon the Father in Heaven, He means to remind you of our beautiful fatherland. And by thus putting into your mind a stronger desire for these good things, He sets you on the way that will lead you back to your original country.

Now the way which leads human nature back to Heaven is none other than that of avoiding the evils of the world by flight; on the other hand, the purpose of fleeing from evils seems to me precisely to achieve likeness with God.[44] To become like God means to become just, holy, and good and suchlike things. If anyone, as far as in him lies, clearly shows in himself the characteristics of these virtues, he will pass automatically and without effort from this earthly life to the life of Heaven. For the distance between the Divine and the human is not a local one so as to need some mechanical device by which this heavily weighted earthly flesh should migrate into the disembodied intelligible life. No; if virtue has really been separated from evil, it lies solely within the free choice of man to be there where his desire inclines him. Since, therefore, the choice of the good is not followed by any labour—for possession of the things that are chosen follows the act of choice—you are entitled to be in Heaven immediately, because you have seized God with your mind. Now if, according to Ecclesiastes, *God is in Heaven*,[45] and you, according to the Prophet, *adhere to God*,[46] it follows necessarily that you should be where God is, because you are united to Him. Since then He has commanded in the prayer to call God Father, He tells you to do nothing less than to become like to your Heavenly Father by a life that is worthy of God, as He bids us do more clearly elsewhere when He says: *Be you therefore perfect, as also your Heavenly Father is perfect.*[47]

If we have now understood the meaning of the prayer, it may perhaps be time to prepare our souls so that we may pronounce the words with bold confidence: *Our Father, who art in Heaven.* For as there are obvious characteristics of resemblance to God through which one may become a child of God (for He says: *As many as received Him, He gave them power to be made the sons of God* [48] —but he who receives the perfect good receives God); so also there are certain signs belonging to the evil character the bearer of which cannot be the son of God, because he is stamped with the image of the contrary nature.[49] Would you like to know the features of the evil character? They are envy and hate, slander, conceit, cupidity, passionate lust and mad ambition. By these and similar signs the form of the adversary is recognized. If then a man whose soul is impregnated with such stains shall call upon his father, what kind of a father will hear him? Evidently one who is akin to the man who calls upon him; and this is not the heavenly, but the infernal father. For the one who bears the family features will surely recognize his own kind. Therefore as long as the evil man persists in his wickedness, his prayer is an invocation of the devil. But when he has abandoned his wickedness and is living a good life, then his words will call upon the Father who is good. For this reason, before we approach God we should first examine our life, if we have something worthy of the Divine kinship in ourselves, and so we may make bold to use such a word.

For He who has commanded us to say Father, has not permitted us to pronounce a lie. He, therefore, who lives in a manner worthy of the Divine nobility, has the right to look towards the Heavenly City, calling the King of Heaven his Father and the celestial beatitude his fatherland. For what is the purpose of this counsel? That one should think of the things that are above, where God is. There should be laid the foundations of the house, there the treasures should be stored, there the heart should be settled. *For where the treasure is, there is also the heart.*[50] We should always look at the beauty of the Father and fashion the beauty of our own soul on His.

There is no respect of persons with God, says the Scripture.[51] Let your beauty also be without this blemish. The Divine is pure from envy and from all stain of passion. Therefore let no such passions defile you, neither envy nor vanity nor any of those things that would pollute the Divine Beauty. If such is what you are, you may boldly address God by a familiar name and call the Lord of all your Father. He will look upon you with the eyes of a Father, He will clothe you with the Divine robe and adorn you with a ring; He will shoe your feet for the upward journey with the sandals of the Gospel and will restore you to the Heavenly Fatherland, in Christ Jesus Our Lord, to whom be glory and power for ever and ever. Amen.

SERMON 3

Hallowed be Thy Name, Thy Kingdom come.

The Law having a shadow of the good things to come [52] prefigures the truth in types and allegories. When it introduces the priest into the Holy of Holies in order to pray to God, it purges him before entering by purifying aspersions. It then puts on him the priestly robe beautifully decked with gold, purple, and other brilliant colourings, places the girdle round his breast and suspends the pomegranates from the borders hung with bells. It then fastens the tunic on his shoulders, adorns his head with a diadem, lavishes ointment on his hair, [53] and thus brings him into the Holy of Holies to perform the sacred rites.

But the spiritual Lawgiver, Our Lord Jesus Christ, strips the Law of its material veils and lays bare the types and allegories. First of all, He does not give communion with God only to one whom He separates from everyone else, but He bestows this honour equally on all, offering the grace of the priesthood as common to those who desire it. Secondly, He does not manufacture the priestly beauty from alien adornments produced from dyes and curious devices of weaving, but He puts on him his own native adornments, decking him with the graces of virtue rather than with an embroidered purple robe. Not with earthly gold does He adorn his breast, but his very heart He makes beautiful through a perfectly pure conscience. He also fits the diadem with the rays coming from precious stones;

they are the lustre of the holy commandments, according to the Apostle. He also covers with breeches that part of the body which is adorned by this garment;[54] for you surely know that this part is clothed with the covering of chastity. As to the spiritual pomegranates and bells which He suspends from the borders of life, these one might rightly conceive to be the evidence of virtuous living by which such way of life may become widely known. In the place of the bells, therefore, He suspends from the borders the melodious word of the faith; instead of the pomegranates the hidden preparation of the future hope still covered over by the more material bodily life instead of the flowers, the glorious gift of paradise; and thus He leads him to the *adyton*,[55] that is, to the innermost part of the Temple.

This *adyton* is not inanimate nor made by hands; but it is the hidden inner chamber of our heart if it be truly *adyton* (impenetrable) to evil and inaccessible to vile thoughts. The head, too, He adorns, not with the shape of letters embossed with gold leaf, but with a heavenly mind on the highest faculty of which, that is to say, reason, God Himself is impressed.[56] Ointment He pours on his hair distilled from the interior virtues of the soul. A sacrificial victim, too, He prepares for him to offer to God in the mystic[57] rite, which is none other than Himself. Being thus led by the Lord to this sacrifice, he mortifies his fleshly mind with *the sword of the spirit, which is the word of God*,[58] and thus appeases God. Being in the *adyton*, he immolates himself in such a sacrifice, *presenting his body a living sacrifice, holy—pleasing unto God*.[59]

But someone might perhaps say that this is not the obvious meaning of the prayer we are interpreting; that we are wangling the words and fail to adapt our interpretation to the text before us. Therefore it should be remembered what we have said about prayer before. We said that he who has prepared himself so that he may boldly call God his Father is precisely he who is clad in such a robe as described in this sermon. He rings with bells and is adorned with pomegranates; his breast shines with the rays of the commandments and he bears on his shoulders the patriarchs and prophets themselves instead of only their names; for he has made their virtues his own adornment. He has placed on his head the crown of justice and soaked his hair with heavenly ointment; he dwells in the supercelestial *adyta* which are *adyta* to all profane thought and truly inaccessible.

But by briefly examining this, the sermon has sufficiently shown how a man ordained to the priesthood should be prepared; now there remains to consider the petition itself which the person within the sanctuary has been ordered to offer to God. For in my opinion the words of the prayer that are so concisely proposed to us do not yield a meaning that can easily be understood at first sight.

Hallowed be Thy Name, He says, *Thy Kingdom come*. What has this to do with my needs?—somebody might say who is doing penance because he repents of his sins or invokes the help of God in order to escape from his besetting weakness, because he is always aware of the temptations of the enemy. For on the one hand, fits of anger upset reasonable moderation; on the other, unnatural lusts enervate the soul's strength; from yet another direction covetousness blinds the clear sight of the soul; conceit, pride, hatred, and the rest of the catalogue of the forces fighting against us encircle us like a hostile army and endanger the final destiny of the soul. Now if a man is anxious to enlist the help of a Stronger One in order to escape from these dangers, what words would he be likely to use? Not those of the great David—*Deliver me from them that hate me,*[60] and, *Let my enemies be turned back,*[61] and, *Give us help from trouble,*[62] and similar petitions by which one may procure God's help against one's enemies? What, however, says the pattern of prayer? *Hallowed be Thy Name.* Now even if I did not say that, would it be at all possible that God's name should not be holy? *Thy Kingdom come.* What is there that is not subject to the power of God, who, as Isaias says, holds the whole heaven in His palm, who compasses the earth, whose hand rules the moist nature,[63] who embraces the whole mundane and supramundane creation? But if the name of God is always holy, and nothing escapes His powerful dominion; if He rules all things, and nothing can be added to His holiness, since He is in all things absolutely perfect—what does it mean to pray: *Hallowed be Thy Name, Thy Kingdom come?* Perhaps by using such form of prayer the Word intends to set forth something like this: namely that human nature is too weak to achieve anything good, and that therefore we can obtain nothing of the things for which we are anxious unless the good be accomplished in us by Divine aid. And of all good things the most important for me is that God's name should be glorified through my life. But perhaps our meaning will become clearer if we start from the opposite end.

I have heard Holy Scripture somewhere condemn those who are guilty of blaspheming God. *Woe to those,* it says, *through whom my Name is blasphemed among the Gentiles.*[64] Now the meaning of these words is something like this: Those who have not yet believed the word of truth closely examine the lives of those who have received the mystery of the faith. If, therefore, people are "faithful" only in name, but contradict this name by their life, whether by committing idolatry for the sake of gain or by disgracing themselves by drunkenness and revelry, being immersed in profligacy like swine in the mud—then the pagans immediately attribute this not to the free choice of these evil-living men, but to the mystery [65] which is supposed to teach these things. For, they say, such and such a man who has been initiated into the Divine mysteries would not be such a slanderer, or so avaricious and grasping, or anything equally evil, unless sinning was lawful for them. Therefore the Word holds out a grave threat to such men, saying to them: *Woe to those through whom my Name is blasphemed among the Gentiles.*

Now if this has been properly understood, it will be time to consider the opposite. For I think it is necessary to make this before all else the principal part of prayer that the Name of God might not be blasphemed, but hallowed and glorified through my life. The prayer says, in effect, let the Name of His dominion which I invoke be hallowed in me, *that men may see your good works and glorify your Father who is in Heaven.*[66] Who would be so absurdly unreasonable as not to glorify God if he sees in those who believe in Him a pure life firmly established in virtue? I mean a life purged from all stain of sin, above any suspicion of evil and shining with temperance and holy prudence. A man who leads such a life will oppose fortitude to the assaults of the passions; since he partakes of the requirements of life only as far as necessary, he is in no way softened by the luxuries of the body and is an utter stranger to revelry and laziness as well as to boastful conceit. He touches the earth but lightly with the tip of his toes, for he is not engulfed by the pleasurable enjoyments of its life, but is above all deceit that comes by the senses. And so, even though in the flesh, he strives after the immaterial life. He counts the possession of virtues the only riches, familiarity with God the only nobility. His only privilege and power is the mastery of self so as not to be a slave of human passions. He is saddened if his life in this material world be prolonged; like those who are seasick he hastens to reach the port of rest.

How could anyone who sees such a man fail to glorify the Name invoked by such a life? Therefore if I pray *Hallowed be Thy Name*, I ask that these words may effect in me things such as these: May I become through Thy help blameless, just and pious, may I abstain from every evil, speak the truth, and do justice. May I walk in the straight path, shining with temperance, adorned with incorruption, beautiful through wisdom and prudence. May I meditate on the things that are above and despise what is earthly, showing forth the angelic way of life. These and similar things are comprised in this brief petition by which we pray to God: *Hallowed be Thy Name*. For a man can glorify God in no other way save by his virtue which bears witness that the Divine Power is the cause of his goodness.

In the following clause we pray that God's Kingdom should come. Could this really mean that He who *is* King of the universe should *become* King? He who is always the same and incapable of change, since He could not find anything better into which to change? What, then, does this prayer mean that asks for the Kingdom of

God? Its true significance may be known to those to whom the Spirit of truth reveals hidden mysteries. Our own interpretation of the saying is this: There is one true and perfect power which is above all things and governs the whole universe. But it rules not by violence and tyrannical dictatorship, which enforces the obedience of its subjects through fear and compulsion. For virtue must be free from the fear of a taskmaster, so as to choose the good by a voluntary act; since it is a principle that all that is good should be subject only to the power that gives life.

Now since man's nature was deceitfully led astray from the discernment of the good, the inclination of his free will has been directed to the opposite and his life subjected to every base thing; his nature has been mixed up with death in a thousand ways, for every form of evil is, as it were, a way of death for him. Since, then, we are hard pressed by such tyranny and become slaves to death through the assaults of the passions, which attack us like executioners and enemies in war, we rightly pray that the Kingdom of God may come to us. For we cannot escape the wicked dominion of corruption except the lifegiving power take over the government in its place.

So if we ask that the Kingdom of God may come to us, the meaning of our request is this: I would be a stranger to corruption and liberated from death; would that I were freed from the shackles of sin and that death no longer lorded it over me. Let us no more be tyrannized by evil so that the adversary may not prevail against me and make me his captive through sin. But may Thy Kingdom come to me, so that the passions which still rule me so mercilessly may depart from me, or rather may be altogether annihilated. For *As smoke vanisheth, so shall they vanish*

away; and *as wax melteth . . . , so shall they perish.*[67]
The smoke which dissolves in the air leaves no trace of its
existence, nor can wax be found any more once it has been
in the fire. But as the latter, having nourished the flame
with its own substance, has evaporated into the air, and as
the smoke has disappeared into complete nothingness, so,
when the Kingdom of God comes upon us, all the things
that now hold sway will cease to exist. Thus darkness
vanishes before the presence of light, and illness passes
when health has been established. The passions cease to
be troublesome when *apatheia* [68] has appeared; death is un-
done and corruption is no more when life and incorruption
reign in us unopposed.

Thy Kingdom come. By this sweet word we obviously
offer God this prayer: Let the opposing battle front be
broken and the hostile phalanx be destroyed. Bring to an
end the war of the flesh against the spirit and let the body
no longer harbour the enemy of the soul. Oh, let them
appear, the royal force, the angelic band, the thousands of
rulers, the myriads of those who stand on Thy right hand,
that a thousand warriors may fall on the front of the enemy! Strong, indeed, is the adversary, formidable, yea,
invincible to those bereft of Thy help. Yet only as long
as man is fighting alone; when Thy Kingdom comes, the
pangs and sighs of sorrow vanish, and life, peace, and rejoicing enter instead.

Perhaps the same thought is expressed more clearly for
us by Luke, who, when he desires the Kingdom to come,
implores the help of the Holy Spirit. For so he says in
his Gospel; instead of *Thy Kingdom come* it reads "May
Thy Holy Spirit come upon us and purify us." [69] What
will the impertinent wordmongers say to these words on

the Holy Spirit? [70] By which trick of exegesis will they change the dignity of the Kingdom into the lowliness of servitude? For what Luke calls the Holy Spirit, Matthew calls the Kingdom; how then do these enemies of God [71] drag Him down into a subject creature, placing Him with the ruled, instead of with the ruling Nature? The creature's property is to serve; and service is not kingship. But the Holy Spirit is kingship.[72] Therefore He is separated from the common being of creatures. For he who rules is not ruled; and he who is not ruled, is not a creature.

The characteristic of the creature is to serve. If therefore the Holy Spirit is kingship, how do they refuse to acknowledge His sovereignty—those people who have not even learned how to pray? They do not even know who it is that purifies what is defiled; who is endowed with the authority of kingship.

"May Thy Holy Spirit come," he says, "and purify us." Therefore the proper power and virtue of the Holy Spirit is precisely to cleanse sin; for what is pure and undefiled needs no cleansing. Now the very same thing the Apostle says also about the Only-Begotten, who, *making purgation of our sins, sitteth on the right hand of the majesty* of the Father.[73] Therefore the same is the work of either, of the Spirit who cleanses from sin as well as of Christ who has made the purgation. But if two perform the same operation, then their power must also be exactly the same, for every operation is the effect of power. If then there is one operation as well as one power, how can one assume a diversity of nature in those in whom we can find no difference of power and operation? For as in the properties of fire, since the two—illuminating and burning—are quite similar, there cannot be held to be a change of subject, so neither will a wise man be led to conjecture a difference of nature in the Son and the Spirit, because he has been taught by the Divine Scripture that they have the same operation.

But now it has already been shown by the arguments of godly men [74] that the nature of the Father and the Son is the same, that it is impossible to call by the name of God what is of different nature. For the son of a carpenter is not called a bench, nor would any person in his right mind say that an architect had begot the house; but the names of the Son and the Father signify what is joined together in the same nature. Now it is absolutely necessary, if two are by nature conjoined to one, that they are in no wise different from each other. That is to say, if the Son is by nature united to the Father, and if the Holy Spirit has been shown not to be alien from the nature of the Son on account of the identity of operations, it necessarily follows, I say, that the nature of the Holy Trinity has been shown to be one, though not confused as regards the properties which belong to each Person as His special characteristic, since their special features are not changed into each other. Hence [75] the characteristic of the Father's Person [76] cannot be transferred to the Son or the Spirit, nor, on the other hand, can that of the Son be accommodated to one of the others, or the property of the Spirit be attributed to the Father and the Son. But the incommunicable distinction of the properties is considered in the common nature. It is the characteristic of the Father to exist without cause. This does not apply to the Son and the Spirit; for the Son *went out from the Father,*[77] as says the Scripture, and *the Spirit proceedeth* from God and *from the Father.*[78] But as the being without cause, which belongs only to the Father, cannot be adapted to the Son and the Spirit, so again the being caused, which is the property of the Son and of the Spirit, cannot, by its very nature, be considered in the Father. On the other hand, the being not ungenerated is common to the Son and the Spirit; hence in order to avoid confusion in the subject, one must again search for the pure difference in the properties, so that what is common be safeguarded, yet what is proper be not mixed. For He is called the Only-Begotten of the Father by the Holy Scripture; [79] and this term establishes His property for Him. But the Holy Spirit is also said to be from the Father, and is testified to be the Son's. For it says: *If any man have not the Spirit of Christ, he is none of His.*[80] Hence the Spirit that is from God is also Christ's Spirit; but the Son, who is from God, neither is nor is said to be from the Spirit; and this relative sequence is permanent and inconvertible. Hence the sentence cannot properly be resolved and reversed in its meaning so that, as we say the Spirit to be Christ's, we might also call Christ the Spirit's. Since, therefore, this individual property distinguishes one from the other with absolute clarity, but as, on the other hand, the identity of action bears witness to the community of nature, the right doctrine about the Divinity is confirmed in both; namely that the Trinity is numbered by the Persons, but that it is not divided into parts of different nature.

What madness then for these warriors against the Spirit to teach that the Lord is a servant! They do not even consider Paul a trustworthy witness who says *Now the Lord is a Spirit.*[81] Or do they perhaps imagine that the words "May He come" [82] take away His dignity? Do they not listen to the great David who would draw also the Father to himself when he cries out, *Come to deliver us?* [83] If, then, in the Father the coming is a saving action, how can it be degrading in the Spirit? Or do they regard the cleansing from sins as a sign of lesser dignity? But listen to the unbelieving Jews who cry that forgiving sins is the prerogative of God, saying with reference to the Father: *Why does this man speak blasphemies? Who can forgive sins but God only?* [84] If therefore the Father forgives sins, the Son takes away the sins of the world, and the Holy Spirit cleanses from the stains of sin those in whom He dwells—what will these fighters against their own life say? But may the Holy Spirit come upon us and purify us and enable us to receive high thoughts worthy of God, which are shown to us by the word of the Saviour; to whom be glory for ever and ever. Amen.

SERMON 4

Thy Will be done, on earth as it is in Heaven. Give us this day our daily bread.

I once heard a medical expert speaking on the subject of health, and what he said may perhaps not be without interest for us in regard to the well-being of the soul. He defined as the principal cause of a state of illness the deviation from the right proportion of one of the elements [85] in us. And, conversely, he said that the cure of the cause of the disease was brought about by restoring the balance that had been viciously disturbed. And therefore he advised that as a contribution to health, care should be taken to weaken those elements in us which were particularly stirred up to disorder by the proper strengthening of the opposing element. For example, if the element of heat is prevalent, one should give help to the oppressed by moistening what is dried up; lest, owing to the absence of fuel, the heat should wither up and be extinguished completely and so be consumed by itself. In the same way one should act also if any of the other opposing elements which are in us exceeds its limits by excessive growth, and give artificial support to what is weakened. If this is done, and nothing prevents the elements from being equally proportioned, the body is restored to health since the natural balance is no longer upset.

But what is the aim of this long introduction to our sermon? Perhaps the consideration is neither without purpose nor far removed from the subject under discussion. The words proposed to our consideration are, *Thy Will be done.* Now why we have called to mind the medical theory, we shall make clear in what follows.

Once upon a time the intelligent human being was healthy, for the movements of the soul, corresponding to the elements, were evenly balanced in us according to the conception of virtue. But when the concupiscent element gained the upper hand, the disposition known to be its opposite, namely continence, was defeated by its stronger enemy, and there was nothing to hinder the inordinate movements of cupidity towards forbidden things. Through this the deadly disease of sin was introduced into human nature. Therefore the true Physician [86] of the diseases of the soul, who shared the life of man for the sake of those who were sick, gradually weakens the cause of disease through the thoughts contained in the prayer and so restores us to spiritual health.

Now the health of the soul is the accomplishment of the Divine Will, just as, on the other hand, the disease of the soul that ends in death is the falling away from this good Will. We fell ill when we forsook the wholesome way of life in Paradise and filled ourselves with the poison of disobedience, through which our nature was conquered by this evil and deadly disease. Then there came the true Physician who cured the evil perfectly by its opposite, as is the law of medicine. For those who had succumbed to the disease because they had separated themselves from the Divine Will, He frees once more from their sickness by uniting them to the Will of God. For the words of the prayer bring the cure of the disease which is in the soul. For He prays as if His soul was immersed in pain, saying,

Thy Will be done. Now the Will of God is the salvation of men. If therefore we prepare to say to God: Thy Will be done also in me, it is absolutely necessary first to renounce what was contrary to the Divine Will and to give a full account of it in confession.

For I am meant to say: The will that is opposed to God has worked evil in me throughout my former life, and I have been the servant of the wicked tyrant, carrying out the death sentence against myself like an executioner. Therefore have pity on my misery and give at last that Thy Will may be done in me. As darkness vanishes when light is brought into the gloom of caves, so also, when Thy Will is done in me, every foul and wicked movement of my free will is brought to nought. For continence will extinguish the uncontrolled impulses of a mind dominated by passion; humility will destroy conceit, moderation will heal the disease of pride; whereas the supreme good of charity will expel a whole catalogue of opposing evils from the soul. Before this virtue recede hate and envy, wrath and all angry dispositions of our emotions. It casts out treachery and hypocrisy, brooding over injuries and craving for revenge; it calms the furious beating of the heart and the evil eye. The whole host of such evils is wiped out by a charitable disposition. Thus the Will of God effectively casts out a twofold idolatry; a twofold idolatry, that is to say, that concerning idols, and the greed of silver and gold, which the prophecy calls the idols of the Gentiles.[87] Therefore let Thy Will be done so that the will of the devil may be destroyed.

But why do we pray that the choice of the good may come to us from God? Because human nature, being once enervated by evil, is weak to do the good. For man does not return from evil to good as easily as he turns towards evil. The same principle can be seen also in the case of the body; the sick body is not healed in the same way nor as easily as the healthy body falls ill. Thus a man who has so far been in good health often finds himself in danger of death through just one wound. One fit or attack of fever may destroy the body's strength completely, and one drop of poison will kill altogether or very nearly. The bite of a snake, or the sting of another venomous animal may be followed immediately by illness or death; and the same may happen through a slip or a fall, through overeating or anything else like these. The cure of the illness, on the other hand, is effected only with difficulty through much thought and medical skill, if it be brought about at all. Therefore if we feel an impulse to do evil we need no help; for evil accomplishes itself in our will. But if there is an inclination towards something good, we need God to carry the desire into effect. Therefore we say: Because Thy Will is temperance, but I am carnal and sold under sin, may this good Will be accomplished in me by Thy power; and so it is also with justice, piety, and deliverance from the passions. For the word "will" contains generically all the virtues; and all the individual things that are understood by the word "good" are contemplated in the Will of God.

But what means the additional clause, *on earth as it is in Heaven?* It seems to me that the words indicate perhaps one of the more profound doctrines, and contain a teaching of the Divine Mind through the contemplation of the creature.

What I mean is this. The whole rational creation is divided into the incorporeal and the corporeal natures.

The incorporeal species is the angelic creature, and the other one is we men. The spiritual creature, inasmuch as it is separated from the body that weighs down—I mean the earthly body that is solid and heavy—sojourns in the upper region. It dwells in the light and ethereal places and is of a nimble and agile nature.[88] But the other nature has necessarily been allotted to the earthly life because of the kinship of our body, which is, as it were, a sediment of mud, with what is earthly. Now I do not know what was the purpose of the Divine Will in so ordering it. Perhaps it was to bring the whole creation into relationship with itself, so that neither the lower portion should be without part in the heavenly heights, nor heaven wholly without a share in the things pertaining to earth. Thus the creation of man would effect in each of the elements a participation in the things belonging to the other; for the spiritual nature of the soul, which seems to be decidedly akin to the heavenly powers, dwells in earthly bodies, and in the restoration of all,[89] this earthly flesh will be translated into the heavenly places together with the soul. As the Apostle says, *We . . . shall be taken up . . . in the clouds to meet the Lord, into the air, and so shall we be always with the Lord.*[90] Hence, whether the wisdom of God intend this or anything else besides, every rational nature is assigned to one of these two lives: the one, incorporeal, obtains the heavenly beatitude; whereas the other is turned towards the earth because of the affinity between it and the flesh.

Yet the desire for the good and the beautiful [91] is equally inherent in both natures, and the Lord of the world has both equally endowed with self-determined free will and complete freedom from necessity. Thus, every being privileged to possess a rational mind is meant to be governed by an autonomous free will. Now the heavenly life is perfectly free from evil, and none of the powers known to be opposed to it has communion with it. On the other hand, every impulse or emotion connected with the passions resides in the life below, where human nature is at home. Therefore the Divinely inspired Word fixes the attention on the heavenly city, the dwelling place of the holy powers, which is perfectly free from even the slightest stain of sin and evil. But whatever has placed itself outside the good through its own secession from it, has an admixture of evil in its substance; and it flows together in this life like new bad wine and dregs in a basin. Thus mankind is contaminated, for such darkness prevents it from beholding the Divine Light of Truth.

Since, then, the life above is passionless and pure, whereas this wretched life here below is immersed in all manner of passions and miseries, it should be clear that the city above, being pure from all evil, is firmly established in the good Will of God. For where there is no evil there must necessarily be the good. But our life, which has fallen away from sharing the good things, has at the same time fallen away from the Divine Will. Therefore the prayer teaches us thus to purify our life from evil that the will of God may rule in us without hindrance, in the same way as it does in the life of heaven. In other words: As Thy Will is done by the thrones and principalities and powers and dominations [92] and all the supramundane hosts, where no evil hinders the action of the good, so may the good be accomplished also in us. Thus, when all evil has been removed, Thy Will may be accomplished in our souls in all things.

But someone might suggest an objection: How can those who have been destined for life in the flesh achieve the purity which is in the disembodied spirits? Do not the needs of the body plunge the soul into a thousand cares? Therefore I propose to solve this problem whilst dealing with the apparent difficulty in the next part of the subject under discussion.

For I believe that a definite doctrine is presented to us in these words, in that we are commanded to ask for our daily bread; that is to say, the nature that is temperate and content with little according to the idea of *apatheia* should be made equal to the nature that has no material needs at all. The angel does not pray to God for sufficient bread, because his nature has no need of such things. But man is commanded to ask this, because what is empty certainly needs to be filled. For the human life is constituted unstable and transitory, seeking to renew itself by supplying for what it loses. A man, therefore, who gives but nature its due and does not let his vain thoughts stray after things outside his needs is not far below the angelic state: he imitates their need of nothing as far as in him lies by being content with little. Therefore we have been commanded to seek only what is sufficient to preserve our physical existence.

So we say to God: Give us bread. Not delicacies or riches, nor magnificent purple robes, golden ornaments, precious stones, or silver dishes. Nor do we ask Him for landed estates, or military commands, or political leadership. We pray neither for herds of horses and oxen or other cattle in great numbers, nor for a host of slaves. We do not say, give us a prominent position in assemblies or monuments and statues raised to us, nor silken robes and musicians at meals, nor any other thing by which the soul is estranged from the thought of God and higher things; no—but only bread!

Do you realize the whole scope of the Divine teaching? [93] How much doctrine is not compressed into this short sentence! Does He not clearly proclaim in these words something like this to His listeners: Men, let yourselves no longer be distracted by desiring vanities; stop heaping toil upon toil for yourselves. The needs of your nature are but few; you owe food to your flesh—a trivial thing and easily procured, if you content yourselves with what is necessary. Why do you lay yourselves under so much tribute? Why do you submit to the yoke of paying so many fines? Mining silver, digging gold, and searching for transparent stones—for no other purpose save that your stomach, this perpetual tax collector, may live daintily through all this. Yet it needs only bread to supply the needs of the body. But you go on business to the Indies and venture out upon strange seas; you go on a voyage every year only to bring back flavourings for your food, without realizing that the enjoyment of the spices goes no further than the palate. In the same way the loveliness of sight or smell or taste presents the senses with very transitory delight; except for the palate, there is no difference in the foods consumed, for nature changes all things equally into an evil smell. Do you see the end of fine cookery? Do you realize what are the results of wizard flavourings? Ask for bread because life needs it, and you owe it to the body because of your nature. But all those superfluous things that have been invented by men given to luxury are weeds sown in besides. The seed sown by the Master of the house is corn, from which bread is made.

Luxuries, however, are the tares sown in by the enemy with the wheat. If men refuse to satisfy their nature by what is necessary they are truly choked, as Scripture says somewhere, by the pursuit of vanities; [94] for if the soul is perpetually occupied with these things it remains atrophied itself.

I suppose that Moses perhaps teaches something like this by means of symbols, [95] when he presents the serpent as Eve's counsellor in matters of taste. People say that this animal—I mean the serpent—cannot easily be drawn back by its tail, if one is trying to pull it in the opposite direction while it is crawling, head foremost, through a chink. For the sharp scales of its back naturally resist the force of those that are pulling it. Hence, whereas it can glide forward unhindered because the scales slide along smoothly, it is impossible to draw it out from the back, because the resisting scales prevent it. Thus Scripture, it seems to me, shows that one must beware of lust sneaking into the soul from the back, and that one has to block up as far as possible the "chinks" presented by the life of the body. Only thus can the spiritual life of man be preserved pure from the society of beasts. [96] For if these gain access to us, because the balance of our life has been upset, [97] the serpent of lust sneaks in through the chinks and is difficult to dislodge from the precincts of the mind because of the scales.

Now by the metaphor of the scales we must understand the manifold occasions of lust. For, speaking generally, the passion of lust is but one animal; but the many various forms of lust which are intermingled with the human life through the senses are the scales surrounding the serpent, speckled by the various passion-provoking incidents. If, therefore, you wish to avoid having to live with the beast, beware of its head, that is, of the first assault of evil; for this is the meaning of the Lord's symbolic command: *He shall lie in wait for your heel, and you shall lie in wait for his head.*[98] Do not give access to the reptile creeping into the inner chamber, for its whole trail enters with it immediately. Cling only to what is necessary; let your care for your livelihood end when you have supplied for your needs by what you can easily obtain. If with you, too, Eve's counsellor converses about what is pleasing to sight and sweet to taste, you will seek over and above your bread this or that flavour, making it more tasty by all manner of seasonings. And through these things which go beyond the range of what is necessary you will bring in desire, and presently you will see the reptile clandestinely creeping towards covetousness. For having once crept from the necessary food towards delicacies, it will proceed to what is pleasant to the eyes, seeking shining dishes and attractive servants. And so on to silver couches, soft divans, and transparent, gold-embroidered veils, magnificent chairs and tripods, washing vessels, mixing bowls, drinking horns, wine coolers and pitchers; water stoups, candlesticks, censers and similar things. And all this serves only to increase the desire for more. For in order that none of these paraphernalia may be missing, one needs an income adequate for providing all these requirements. And so someone must weep, his neighbour must sorrow, many who are deprived of their property must be miserable, in order that their tears may contribute to enhance the ostentatious display of his table. And when the serpent has wound its coils about these things and has filled its belly at will, then, as soon as it is sated, it drags itself crawling down to unbridled frenzy. This is the lowest degradation of man.

In order that none of these things may happen, life is defined by bread which is easily obtainable, for which you may seek the flavouring that is provided by nature itself. This is above all a good conscience which makes the bread tasty because it is eaten in justice. But if you want to enjoy also the physical sense of taste, let hunger be your flavouring; do not overeat yourself so that you have no appetite because you are feeling sick. But let the sweat mentioned in the commandment precede your meal—*In sweat and labour shalt thou eat thy bread.*[99] You see this is the first kind of flavour Scripture mentions.

It will be enough for you to reflect as far as this need. Rather, do not even entangle your soul thus far in the care for bread; but say to Him who *brings bread out of the earth,*[100] say to Him who nourishes the ravens [101] and *gives food to all flesh,*[102] to Him *who opens His hand and fills with blessing every living creature:* [103] My life I have from Thee—from Thee let me also have the needs of life. Give Thou bread—that is to say, let me have food through just labour. For if God is justice, the man who procures himself food through covetousness cannot have his bread from God. You are the master of your prayer, if abundance does not come from another's property and is not the result of another's tears; if no one is hungry or distressed because you are fully satisfied. For the bread of God is above all the fruit of justice, the ear of the corn of peace, pure and without any admixture of the seed of tares. But if you cultivate what is another's property, if you practise injustice and confirm your unjust gains by written documents, then you may indeed say to God: Give bread; but another will hear this your plea, not God. For the fruit of injustice is the product of the contrary nature. He who pursues righteousness receives his bread from God, whereas the man who cultivates iniquity is fed by the father of iniquity.[104]

Therefore look into your own conscience before you ask God for bread; for you know that Christ has no company with Belial.[105] But if you offer gifts of iniquity, they are the purchase money of a dog, the price of a prostitute. Even if you distinguish yourself by costly gifts, listen how the prophet abominates such offerings: *To what purpose do you offer me the multitude of your victims? saith the Lord. I am full of holocausts of rams and I desire not fat of fatlings and blood of calves and lambs. . . . Incense, He says, is an abomination to me.*[106] In another passage[107] someone who sacrifices a sheep is compared to one who kills a dog. If, however, you have your bread from the Lord, that is to say, through just labour, you may rightly offer Him of the fruits of justice.

Full of meaning is also the addition of *this day*, when He says: *Give us this day our daily bread.* These words contain yet another teaching.[108] For you should learn through what you say that the human life is but the life of a day. Only the present each one of us can call his own; the hope of the future is uncertain, for we know not *what the day to come may bring forth.*[109] Why then do we make ourselves miserable worrying about the future? He says, *Sufficient for the day is the evil thereof,*[110] evil here meaning the enduring of evil. Why are we disturbed about the morrow? By the very fact that He gives you the commandment for today, He forbids you to be solicitous for the morrow. He says to you as it were: He who gives you the day will give you also the things necessary for the day. Who causes the sun to rise? Who makes the darkness of the night disappear? Who shows you the rays of light? Who revolves the sky so that the source of light is above the earth? Does He who gives you so great things need your help to supply for the needs of your flesh? Do animals take care for their livelihood? Do ravens have tilled land or eagles barns? Is not the one means of providing a livelihood for all the Will of God, by which all things are governed? Therefore even an ox or an ass, or any other animal is taught its way of life by instinct, and it manages the present well but does not concern itself in the least with what comes afterwards. And should we need special advisers in order to understand that the life of the flesh is perishable and transitory? Are we not taught by the misfortunes of others, not chastened by those of our own life?

What profits this rich man his wealth? Like a fool he chases vain hopes, pulling down, building up, hoarding and dissipating, shutting up long periods of years as it were in barns, without letting them bear fruit. Will not one night prove false all these imagined hopes, like some vain dream about a nonentity? The life of the body belongs only to the present, but that which lies beyond us and is apprehended by hope belongs to the soul. Yet men in their folly are quite wrong about the use of either; they would extend their physical lives by hope, and draw the life of the soul towards enjoyment of the present. Therefore the soul is occupied by the world of sense and necessarily estranged from the subsisting reality of hope. What hope it has leans upon unstable things over which it has no control or authority.

Let us therefore learn from the counsel under consideration what one must ask for today, and what for later. Bread is for our use today; the Kingdom belongs to the beatitude for which we hope. By bread He means all our bodily requirements. If we ask for this, the man who prays will clearly understand that he is occupied with something transitory; but if we ask for something of the good things of the soul it will be clear that the petition concerns the everlasting realities, for which He commands us to be most concerned in our prayers. Thus the first necessity is put in its right place by the greater one. *Seek ye*, He says, *the kingdom and justice, and all these things shall be added unto you;* [111] in Christ Jesus Our Lord, to whom be glory and power for ever and ever. Amen.

Forgive us our debts, as we also forgive our debtors.
And lead us not into temptation. But deliver us from evil.

As our enquiry progresses, it comes to the very peak of
virtue; for the words of the prayer outline what sort of a
man one should be if one would approach God. Such
man is almost no longer shown in terms of human nature,
but, through virtue, is likened to God Himself, so that he
seems to be another god, in that he does those things that
God alone can do. For the forgiving of debts [112] is the
special prerogative of God, since it is said, *No man can
forgive sins but God alone.*[113] If therefore a man imitates
in his own life the characteristics of the Divine Nature, he
becomes somehow that which he visibly imitates. What
therefore does the prayer teach? First that we should be
conscious of our likeness to God through the liberty of
our life,[114] then to be bold to call God our Father, and to
ask that our sins should no more be remembered. Not,
indeed, as if it lay with him who asks to obtain his desire,
but that his works have given him boldness to make this
request.

This we are plainly told in the present passage. If
we approach the Benefactor, we should ourselves be
benefactors; if we go to Him who is good and just, we
should ourselves be the same. Because He is forbearing
and kind, we should also be forbearing and kind, and so
with all the other things. For He is benign and gentle,

He communicates good things and dispenses mercy to every one—to all these qualities, and whatever else we may see in the Divine Being, we should be assimilated by our free will. Thus a man should obtain the confidence presupposed by the prayer. It is impossible that a wicked man should be intimate with a good man, or that someone wallowing in impure thoughts should be friends with somebody who is perfectly pure. Thus too a callous man trying to approach God is far from the Divine charity. Hence someone who cruelly detains a man who is in his power on account of debts, separates himself from the Divine kindness by his very way of life. For what communion has kindness with cruelty, a loving character with ferocity?

And so it is with the other things; whatever is known as diametrically opposed to evil cannot be mixed with its opposite; whoever is in the power of the one is completely separated from its contrary. For he who is dead is not alive; and if he enjoys life he is separated from death. Therefore it is absolutely necessary that a man who approaches the charity of God should rid himself of all callousness. And if a man is free from everything that comes under the idea of evil he becomes, so to speak, a god by his very way of life, since he verifies in himself what reason finds in the Divine Nature.

Do you realize to what height the Lord raises His hearers through the words of the prayer, by which He somehow transforms human nature into what is Divine? For he lays down that those who approach God should themselves become gods. Why, He says, do you go to God crouching with fear like a slave because your conscience pricks you? Why do you shut out holy audacity which is inherent in the freedom of the soul because it has been joined to its very essence from the beginning? Why do you seek to flatter with words Him who brooks no flattery? Why do you offer language of abject servility to Him who regards only deeds? Yet you may lawfully say whatever is worthy of God, because your mind is free in its own right. Be yourself your own judge, give yourself the sentence of acquittal. Do you want your debts to be forgiven by God? Forgive them yourself, and God will ratify it. For your judgement of your neighbour which is in your power, whatever it may be, will call forth the corresponding sentence upon you. What you decide for yourself will be confirmed by the Divine judgement.

But how could anyone worthily expound the lofty character of the Divine utterance? The meaning surpasses the exegesis of the words, *Forgive us our debts, as we also forgive our debtors.* It is rash to ponder in my mind the thoughts about it that come into my head, and even more so to reveal what I think in words.

What is actually being said? As to those who would achieve goodness, God is proposed for imitation according to the words of the Apostle, *Be ye followers of me, as I also am of Christ,*[115] so conversely He wants your disposition to be a good example to God! The order is somehow reversed; just as in us the good is accomplished by imitating the Divine goodness, so we dare to hope that God will also imitate us when we accomplish anything good—so that you, too, may say to God: Do Thou the same as I have done. Imitate Thy servant, O Lord, though he be only a poor beggar and thou art the King of the universe. I have forgiven the debts, do not Thou demand them back; I have had regard to him who petitioned me, I have sent my debtor away rejoicing, may Thine be done to likewise. Do not sadden him who is under obligation to Thee; but let both give thanks equally to their creditors. May the same forgiveness be ratified by both for both parties, for my debtor and Thine. He is my debtor, I am Thy debtor; may the disposition which I have shown him also prevail with Thee. I have absolved, absolve Thou, too; I have forgiven, forgive Thou also! I have shown great mercy to my neighbour—imitate Thy servant's charity, O Lord!

Yet my sins are graver than the ones he has committed against me. I admit that; but take into account how far Thou excellest all in goodness. For Thou art just, therefore Thou wilt give to us who have sinned the mercy that is proportioned to Thy exalted power. I have shown a little charity, for my nature did not contain more; but Thou canst show as much as Thou wilt, for Thy munificence is not hampered by lack of power.

But let us now consider the present clause of the prayer in greater detail, if perhaps through closer consideration we may find there also for ourselves guidance to the sublime life. We will therefore examine what debts human nature owes, and, on the other hand, what debts it is in our power to forgive. For from the knowledge of these a fair perception of the Divine goodness may be derived. Let us therefore start from an account of man's debts towards God.

In the first place, man had to pay a penalty to God because he had separated himself from his Maker and deserted to the enemy, and thus become a runaway and apostate from his natural Master. Secondly, because he had exchanged for the liberty of his free will the wicked slavery of sin, he preferred the tyranny of the power of destruction to the companionship of God. But what greater evil is there than not to look at the beauty of the Creator, and to turn one's eyes towards shameful sin instead? What kind of punishment ought to be assigned to the man who scorns the Divine goodness and prefers the baits of the evil one? Which treatise could enumerate all the sins? The defacing of the Image and the destruction of the Divine impress which was formed in us when we were first created? The loss of the groat,[116] the departure from the table of the Father and the familiarity with the life of vile-smelling swine,[117] the ruin of the precious treasure[118] and whatever other sins both Scripture and our reason show us? Since because of all this mankind is liable to being punished by God, it seems to me that the Word teaches us through the prayer never to speak too boldly to God as if we had a pure conscience, however far from human sins a man might be. For perhaps someone who, like the rich young man, had made the Commandments the rule of his life, might make this an occasion to boast of his conduct and say to God: *All these things have I kept from my youth.*[119] And he might assume that, because he has in no wise offended against the Commandments, the prayer about debts would not be suitable for him, being applicable only to those who have really sinned. He would say that such saying was fitting for someone polluted by adultery, or that a man who from covetousness committed idolatry[120] needs the petition for forgiveness; in short, that for anyone whose conscience had been stained by sin it was right and proper to seek refuge in mercy. And if Elias was so great—or he *among those born of women* who came *in the spirit and power of Elias,*[121] or Peter or Paul or John, or any other of those who are most approved by Divine Scripture—why should he use words that beg pardon for his sins? A man who had no debt of sin?

Let not him who is inclined to such an opinion speak impertinently like that Pharisee who did not even know his own nature. For had he known that he was a human being, he would have learned from Holy Scripture that his nature was by no means pure from defilement, for it says that there cannot be found among men one who lives without stain one day.[122] Let therefore no such thoughts come into the mind of the man who approaches God in prayer. The passage enjoins not to look at the things that have been accomplished but to call to mind the common debt of human nature in which everyone including himself has a share, because he participates in the common lot of man's nature, and to beseech the Judge to grant forgiveness of sins.

For since Adam is, as it were, living in us, we see each and all these garments of skin[123] round our nature, and also the transitory fig leaves of this material life which we have badly sewn together for ourselves after being stripped of our own resplendent garments. For instead of the Divine garments we have put on luxuries and reputation, transitory honours and the quickly passing satisfactions of the flesh, at least as long as we look at this place of distress in which we have been condemned to sojourn. But whenever we turn towards the East[124]—not as if God were only there to be contemplated, for He who is everywhere is not particularly apprehended in any part, since He comprises all things equally, but because our first homeland is in the East; I mean our sojourn in Paradise from which we have fallen, for *God planted a paradise in Eden towards the*

East [125]—when, therefore, we look to the East and recall to our memory how we were cast out from the bright regions of bliss in the East, we shall have reason to utter such prayer. For we live in the shadow of the evil fig tree of material life, and have been cast out from the sight of God. We have deserted to the serpent which eats earth and crawls on it, which moves on its chest and its belly and advises us to do the same—to be occupied with earthly delights, to let our heart be drawn to thoughts grovelling in the dust, and to go on our belly, that is to say, to be occupied with a life of pleasure. Having been wrapped up in these things, let us imitate the Prodigal Son after he had endured the long affliction of feeding the swine. When, like him, we return to ourselves and remember the Heavenly Father, we may rightly use these words: *Forgive us our debts.*

Hence, even though one be a Moses or a Samuel, or any other man of outstanding virtue, in so far as he is a man, he does not consider these words less fitting for himself, seeing that he shares Adam's nature and participates in his exile. For since, as the Apostle says, *in Adam we all die,*[126] the words that are suited to Adam's penance are rightly applied to all who have died with him, so that after we have been granted the remission of our sins we may again be saved by the Lord through grace, as says the Apostle.[127]

Now this has been said so that after considering the more general meaning, one may reflect more closely on the matter before us. But if we seek for the true meaning of the passage, I do not think it necessary that we should refer the sense to what is common to human nature; rather, everyone's conscience is sufficient to make the petition for mercy necessary by his own life. For as our life is lived in this world on many levels, partly in the sphere of soul and intellect, partly in that of the bodily senses, it is difficult, so it seems to me, or even altogether impossible, that one should not at least acquiesce in one sinful passion. For example: Since the life which the body enjoys is divided into our senses, but that of the soul is regarded as the impulse given by the mind and the movement of the free will—who is of so surpassingly noble character as to remain free from the stain of evil in both? Whose eye is without sin, whose sense of hearing without reproach? Who is a stranger to the brutish pleasure of gluttony, who is pure from the sins occasioned by touch? Who does not understand the symbolic sense of the Scriptural saying, *Death is come in through the windows?* [128] What Scripture calls windows are the senses, through which the soul issues forth to the things outside and lays hold of those it likes; and thus these windows, as the passage says, make an entrance for death. Truly, the eye is often an entry for many a death. If it sees someone angry, it is incited to the same passion; if it observes one enjoying greater prosperity than he deserves, it burns with envy. It may see someone arrogant and rage with hatred, something of lovely colour or beautiful shape and be completely carried away with desire for the pleasing object. So the ear, too, opens windows to death. Through what it hears it admits many passions into the soul: fear, sorrow, wrath, pleasure, desire, bursts of laughter, and suchlike things. And the pleasure of taste is, one may well say, the mother of each individual evil. For who does not know that indulgence of the palate is pretty nearly the root of the sins committed in the physical life? For on this depend luxury and drunkenness, gluttony and prodigality of table, filling oneself up to satiety and revelling until one sinks into the depths of shameful passions like irrational brutes. Likewise the sense of touch is the last of the senses by which sin can be committed. For all things that pleasure-lovers practise on the body are diseases of the perception of touch, which it would take too long to enumerate in detail. Nor would it be seemly to get all the sins of touch entangled with our serious considerations.

But as to the swarm of sins of the soul and of free will, what sermon could enumerate them? *From within*, He says, *proceed evil thoughts*,[129] and He adds a catalogue of thoughts that defile us. If, therefore, the nets of sin are thus spread around us on every side, through all the senses and through the interior movements of the soul, *Who shall glory*, as Wisdom says, *that his heart is clean?* [130] Or, as Job testifies to the same, *Who is clear from filth?* [131] Filth on the purity of the soul is sensual pleasure,[132] which is mixed up with human life in manifold ways, through soul and body, through thoughts and senses, through deliberate movements and bodily actions.

Whose soul, then, is pure from this stain? How has anyone not been struck by vanity or been trodden down by the foot of pride? Who has never been shaken by the sinning hand, or whose feet have never run to evil? Who has not been polluted by his roving eye nor been defiled by an undisciplined ear? Whose taste has never been preoccupied by its enjoyment, whose heart has remained unmoved by vain emotions?

Now it is true the things before us are much more grievous in more barbarous people and more moderated in those who are more cultivated; yet all those who share a nature most certainly also have a share in the faults of this nature; hence, when we approach God in prayer, we ask that our debts may be forgiven us. But such words are ineffectual and do not reach the Divine hearing unless our conscience cries in unison with us that it is good to impart mercy. For if a man really believes that it is worthy of God to love men—for unless he thought so he would not want to approach Him with something entirely unsuitable —he ought to confirm his judgement on what is good by his own works. Else he might hear from the just Judge words such as these, *Physician, heal thyself.*[133] You ask me to love men, and yourself do not give love to your neighbour? You ask to have debts forgiven, how can you strangle your debtor? You pray that I may blot out what is written against you, and you preserve carefully the acknowledgements of those who owe you something? You ask to have your debts cancelled, but you increase what you have lent by taking interest? Your debtor is in prison, while you are in church?[134] He is in distress on account of his debts, but you think it right that your debt should be forgiven? Your prayer cannot be heard because the voice of him who suffers is drowning it. If you remit the material debt, the bonds of your soul will also be loosened; if you pardon, you will be pardoned. You must be your own judge, your own lawgiver. By the disposition you show to him who is under obligation to you you pronounce the judgement of Heaven on yourself.

It seems to me that the Lord teaches the same thing in another saying, where He presents this doctrine in a narrative. In the story there is a certain king who holds a formidable reckoning.[135] He brings his servants to trial, demanding an account from each of his administrators. Now one of the debtors was brought in and obtained charity, for he prostrated himself, and instead of paying the money proffered a humble petition. He then behaved with extreme harshness towards a fellow servant, because of a small debt, and this harshness against his fellow enraged the king. So he commanded the torturers to remove him altogether from the king's house and to prolong his punishment until he had fully paid the appropriate penalty. For truly some few obols are worth very little compared with thousands of talents, that is to say, the debts owed to us compared with our sins against God.

You are no doubt hurt by somebody's arrogant behaviour, or by the wickedness of a servant, or even a plot against your life. Then, in the fury of your heart, you are roused to take revenge for these things, and you think out all sorts of devices to punish those who have caused you pain. You do not consider, when you are burning with anger against your servant, that it is not nature, but power that has divided mankind into servants and masters. For the Lord of the universe has ordained that only the irrational nature should serve man, as the Prophet says: *Thou hast subjected all things under his feet, all sheep and oxen, the birds and the beasts and the fishes.*[136] He even calls them servants, as is stated in the Prophet's words elsewhere: *Who giveth to beasts their food, and herbs for the service of men.*[137] But man He has adorned with the gift of free will. Therefore he who is subject to you by custom and law is yet equal to you in dignity of nature. He is neither made by you, nor does he live through you, nor has he received from you his qualities of body and soul. Why, then, do you get so much worked up to anger against him if he has been lazy, or run away, or perhaps shown you contempt to your face? You ought to look to yourself instead, how you have behaved to your Lord who has made you and caused you to be born, and has given you a share in the marvels of the world.

He set the sun before you for your delight, and gave you all the necessities of life through the elements, through earth and fire and air and water. He bestowed on you the gift of thought, sense perception, and the understanding that is capable of distinguishing between good and evil. How obedient and blameless are you before such a Lord? Have you not revolted against His sovereignty? Have you not run away to sin and exchanged it for the sovereignty of evil? Have you not as far as you were concerned left desolate the house of the Lord and run away from the place where you were appointed to work and keep guard? Moreover, do you not commit the sins mentioned, either by deed, word, or thought, things that ought not to be, of which God who is everywhere and who sees all things, is a witness? As you are such a man, guilty in so many ways, do you really think that you bestow a great gift on your fellow servant if you overlook some of the faults he commits against you? When therefore we are about to offer to God the petition for mercy and forgiveness, we ought to give holy confidence to our conscience by putting forward our life as an advocate of our words, so that we can truly say, *as we forgive our debtors.*

What means the addition that follows immediately after these words? I think that we ought not to pass this over without considering it. We should know for what we are praying, and proffer the petition with our soul rather than with our lips: *Lead us not into temptation, but deliver us from evil.* What, my brethren, do these words mean? It seems to me that the Lord calls the evil one by many different names according to the distinctions between the evil actions. He names him variously devil, Beelzebub, Mammon, prince of this world, murderer of man, evil one, father of lies, and other such things. Perhaps, therefore, here again one of the names devised for him is "temptation," and the juxtaposition of clauses confirms this assumption. For after saying, *Lead us not into temptation,* He adds that we should be delivered from evil, as if both words meant the same. For if a man who does not enter into temptation is quite removed from evil, and if one who has fallen into temptation is necessarily mixed up with evil, then temptation and the evil one mean one and the same thing. What therefore does the exhortation of the prayer teach us? That we should be separated from the things that belong to this world; as somewhere else He says to the disciples: *The whole world is seated in wickedness.*[138] Therefore if a man desires to be free from wickedness, he will necessarily separate himself from the world. For temptation finds no opportunity for touching the soul unless this preoccupation with worldly things be held out to greedy men like a bait on the hook of evil.

But perhaps our meaning may become clearer through other examples. The sea is often dangerous on account of its mighty waves, but not to those who are far removed from it. Fire destroys, but only if inflammable matter is near it. War is full of danger, but only to those who take part in the battle. As, therefore, a man who wants to escape the terrible calamities of war prays not to become involved in it, and another one who fears fire asks not to find himself in such; as a third one who abhors the sea prays that he may not be obliged to go on a voyage; so also he who fears the assault of the evil one should pray that he may not fall into it. But since, as we have said before, Scripture says that the world is seated in wickedness, and as the occasions for temptation arise from worldly preoccupations, therefore if a man prays truly to be delivered from evil, he asks that he may be far from temptation. For no one would swallow the hook unless he had first gulped down the bait in his greed. But let us rise and say to God, *Lead us not into temptation*—that is to say, into the evils of the world—*but deliver us from evil* which holds sway in this world; from which may we be delivered by the grace of Christ, for His is the power and glory with the Father and the Holy Spirit, now and always, and for ever and ever. Amen.

THE BEATITUDES

SERMON 1

*And seeing the multitudes, He went up into a mountain.
And when He was set down, His disciples came unto Him.
And opening His mouth, He taught them, saying: Blessed
are the poor in spirit, for theirs is the Kingdom of Heaven.*

Who among those present is a disciple of the Word,
and sufficiently so to ascend with Him from the low
ground—from superficial and ignoble thoughts to the spiritual mountain of sublime contemplation? This mountain
leaves behind all shadows cast by the rising hills of wickedness; on the contrary, it is lit up on all sides by the rays of
the true light, and from its summit all things that remain
invisible to those imprisoned in the cave [1] may be seen in
the pure air of truth. Now the Word of God Himself,
who calls blessed those who have ascended with Him,
specifies the nature and number of the things that are contemplated from this height. He points them out, as it
were, with His finger; here the Kingdom of Heaven, there
the inheritance of the earth that is above, then mercy, justice, consolation, kinship with the God of all creation, and
the fruit of persecution, that is, to become a friend of God.
And whatever other things there may be visible, the Word
points them out with His finger from the summit of the
mountain, so that hope may contemplate them from the
height of the peak.

Since, then, the Lord ascends the mountain, let us listen to Isaias who cries: *Come, let us go up to the mountain of the Lord.*[2] If we are weak through sin, let our feeble hands and weak knees be strengthened, as the Prophet instructs us.[3] For when we have reached the summit, we shall find Him who heals all illness and languor, who takes up our infirmities and bears our diseases.[4] Let us therefore ascend quickly, so that we may be established with Isaias on the summit of hope and see from this vantage point the good things that the Word shows to those who follow Him to the heights. May God the Word open His mouth also for us, and teach us those things which to hear is bliss. May the beginning of the teaching He pronounces become to us the beginning of contemplation.

Blessed, He says, *are the poor in spirit, for theirs is the Kingdom of Heaven.* Supposing an avaricious man chanced upon a document supplying information of the place of a treasure, but its position was such that it would involve much sweat and labour for anyone wanting to obtain it. Do you think such a man would be discouraged by the difficulties and slow to take his advantage? Would he think the absence of the fatigue his eagerness might bring him, more pleasant than riches? Surely not. But he would summon all his friends to aid him in this enterprise; he would collect the help of a crowd of people from wherever possible, and thus make the hidden treasure his own. This is the treasure, brethren, which the document indicates; but the wealth is hidden in obscurity. Therefore let us, too, who desire the pure gold, use a multitude of hands, that is to say, prayers, so that the treasure may be brought to light, that all may divide it equally, and each may possess it whole. For the distribution of virtue is such that it is shared out to all who seek after it, and yet is wholly present to each, without being diminished by those who share in it. It is true, in the distribution of earthly wealth the man who puts by for himself more than his due, wrongs those who ought to have an equal share with him; for by increasing his own one certainly diminishes the part of the person with whom one shares. Spiritual wealth, on the contrary, does the same as the sun, which communicates itself to all who seek it and is wholly present to each one of them. Since, therefore, every man hopes for the same reward of his labour, let us all co-operate by prayer to obtain what we seek.

Now I say that one must first consider what exactly is beatitude. Beatitude, in my opinion, is a possession of all things held to be good, from which nothing is absent that a good desire may want. Perhaps the meaning of beatitude may become clearer to us if it is compared with its opposite. Now the opposite of beatitude is misery. Misery means being afflicted unwillingly with painful sufferings. The condition of either is therefore diametrically opposed to the other. For it is natural that the man who is called blessed should thoroughly relish the things that are set before him for his enjoyment; whereas it behoves the man who is deemed unhappy to be sorely grieved by his present condition. Now the one thing truly blessed is the Divinity Itself. Whatever else we may suppose It to be, this pure life, the ineffable and incomprehensible good, is beatitude. It is beatitude, this inexpressible beauty which is very grace, wisdom, and power; this true light that is the fount of all goodness, mighty above all else; the one thing lovable which is always the same, rejoicing without end in infinite happiness. Even if one has said about

It all one can, yet one has said nothing worthy of It. For the mind cannot reach that which IS; even if we continue to think ever more sublime thoughts about It, yet no word can express what is meant.

But as He who fashioned man made him in the image of God; in a derived sense that which is called by this name should also be held blessed, inasmuch as he participates in the true beatitude. For as in the matter of physical beauty the original comeliness is in the actually living face, whereas the second place is held by its reflection shown in a picture; so also human nature, which is the image of the transcendent beatitude, is itself marked by the beauty of goodness, when it reflects in itself the blessed features. But since the filth of sin has disfigured the beauty of the image, He came to wash us with His own water, the living water that springs up unto eternal life. And so, when we have put off the shame of sin, we shall be restored once more to the blessed form.[5]

Now an expert painter could tell the ignorant that a face, to be beautiful, must be composed of certain physical features. It must have such and such hair, such and such eyes, a certain shape of eyebrows and form of cheeks, in a word, every detail through which beauty becomes perfect. Thus also He who paints our soul in the likeness of the only Blessed One, describes in words all that produces beatitude; and He says first: *Blessed are the poor in spirit, because theirs is the Kingdom of Heaven.*

But what benefit can we reap from this munificence, if we have not the meaning of the words explained to us? In the medical science, too, many precious and laboriously discovered medicines are quite unprofitable to those who do not know them, until we learn the use of each of them from that science. What, then, is this poverty of spirit through which we come to possess the Kingdom of Heaven? We know from Scripture that there are two kinds of riches, the one to be desired, the other condemned. The riches of virtue are to be pursued, but material wealth is rejected; for the one is gain to the soul, whereas the other is apt to deceive the senses. Therefore the Lord forbids laying up the latter, because it serves only as food for moths and attracts the wiles of burglars.[6] But He commands us to be zealous for spiritual wealth, which the power of corruption does not touch. By mentioning moths and thieves, He showed what destroys the treasures of the soul. Now if poverty is opposed to wealth, one must by way of analogy also teach a twofold poverty, the one to be rejected, the other to be considered blessed. If a person is poor in temperance, in the precious asset of justice, in wisdom or prudence; or if he is found completely lacking in any other of such great treasures, he is most wretched and pitiable, because he is poor in the things of true value. On the other hand, if a man is voluntarily poor in all that has to do with wickedness, if he has no diabolical treasures hidden in his inner chamber, but is fervent in spirit, he lays up for himself the treasure of poverty in evil. He is the man whom the Word presents as enjoying that poverty which is called blessed, whose fruit is the Kingdom of Heaven.

But let us once more get back to this business of the treasure, let us not weary of letting the probing word bring to light what is hidden. *Blessed*, He says, *are the poor in spirit*. This has in some way also been said before, and will now be said again, that the end of the life of virtue is to become like to God.[7] Yet man can by no means whatever imitate the purity that is without passion. For it is simply impossible that the life that is enmeshed in passions should become like the Nature that is impervious to passions. If, therefore, as the Apostle says,[8] the Divine alone is blessed, and man shares in this blessedness through the likeness with God, but if, on the other hand, it is impossible to imitate God, then beatitude is out of the reach of human life.

There are, however, things belonging to the Godhead which are set up for the imitation of those who wish. Now what are these? It seems to me that by poverty of spirit the Word understands voluntary humility. As an example of this the Apostle adduces the poverty of God when he says: *Who for us became poor, being rich, that we through His poverty might be rich.*[9] Now everything else that is being contemplated in the Divine Nature surpasses the limits of human nature; but humility is connatural and as it were a brother to us who walk on the ground, who are composed of earth and again dissolve into earth. If, therefore, you imitate God in what is possible to your nature, you will yourself have put on the blessed form.

But let no one imagine that humility can be achieved easily and without labour. On the contrary, it needs more effort than the practice of any other virtue. Why? Though man had received good seeds, the chief of the opposite seeds—the tares of pride—sown by the enemy of our life, took root while he was asleep. For the same thing by which the devil had caused his own downfall to earth, caused the miserable human race to fling itself down with him into the common ruin; and there is no other evil so harmful to our nature as that which is caused by pride.

Since, therefore, the vice of arrogance is ingrained in almost everyone who shares the human nature, the Lord begins the Beatitudes with this. He removes pride, the root evil, from our character by counselling us to imitate Him who became poor of His own will, who is the truly Blessed One. In this way we may, as far as we are able, become like Him by being poor of our own free will, and so be also drawn to share His Beatitude. *For, as is said, let this mind be in you, which was also in Christ Jesus: who being in the form of God, thought it not robbery to be equal with God; but emptied Himself, taking the form of a servant.*[10] What greater poverty is there for God than the form of a servant? What more humble for the King of creation than to share in our poor nature? The Ruler of rulers, the Lord of lords puts on voluntarily the garb of servitude. The Judge of all things becomes a subject of governors; the Lord of creation dwells in a cave; He who holds the universe in His hands finds no place in the inn, but is cast aside into the manger of irrational beasts.[11] The perfectly Pure accepts the filth of human nature, and after going through all our poverty passes on to the experience of death. Look at the standard by which to measure voluntary poverty! Life tastes death; the Judge is brought to judgement; the Lord of the life of all creatures is sentenced by the judge; the King of all heavenly powers does not push aside the hands of the executioners. Take this, He says, as an example by which to measure your humility.

But perhaps it may be as well to examine also the absurdity of the contrary vice, so that the beatitude may become effective in us, when humility is established with perfect ease. For as medical experts master a disease more easily by first removing its cause, so we, too, will make the way of humility easier to walk in by first checking the vanity of conceited men through the use of arguments.

How can one best show the emptiness of pride? How, indeed, but by showing nature as it is? For if a man looks at himself rather than at the things around him, he cannot easily fall into such a fault. What, then, is man? Do you wish me to do him honour by giving a rather noble definition? But even if one would flatter our condition and greatly vaunt the human nobility, he will have to trace the pedigree of our nature to clay, and so the high dignity of the proud is related to bricks. But if you should intend to mention the things connected with generation—beware, do not speak nor even whisper about it. Do not, as the Law says,[12] uncover the shame of your father and mother; do not make public what ought to be forgotten and buried in deep silence. Then you will not have to blush, you image of earth that will soon be dust, though you are filled with short-lived conceit like a bubble, and your swollen head is full of pride and burning with vanity on account of your silly ideas. Do you not look at both ends of man's life, where it begins, and how it ends? No, you pride yourself on your youth, you look at the prime of your age and are pleased with your handsome appearance, because your hands can move quickly and your feet are nimble, because your curls are blown about by the breeze and your cheeks show the first signs of a beard. You are proud because your clothes are dyed in brilliant purple and you have silk robes embroidered with scenes from war or hunting or history. Perhaps you also look at your carefully blackened sandals delightfully adorned with elaborate needlework patterns. At these things you look—

but at yourself you will not look? Let me show you as in a mirror who and what sort of a person you are.

Have you never gazed at the mysteries of our nature in a common burial ground? Have you not seen the heaps of bones one on top of the other? Skulls denuded of flesh, fearful and ugly to look at with their empty sockets? Have you not seen their grinning jaws and the other limbs, strewn about at random? If you have seen these things, you have seen yourself. Where will then be today's blooming youth? Where the lovely colour of your cheeks, the fresh lips, the fine brilliance of the eyes flashing under the circle of their brows? What will then have become of the straight nose beautifully set between the cheeks? What of the hair falling down to the neck, and the curls round the temples? Where will be the hands skilled with the bow, the feet controlling the horses? The purple and fine linen, the mantle, the girdle and the sandals? The neighing horses with their race-course? What will have become of all the things that now feed your conceit? Where, in these bones, are all these things about which you are now so greatly puffed up? What dream is so fleeting? What are these hallucinations? What shadow eluding touch is as unsubstantial as the dream of youth that vanishes the moment it appears?

These things I say to those who are foolish in their youth because they are lacking in years. But what shall we say about the middle-aged, who are, indeed, settled in years, but whose moral life is unsettled, and whose pride is a growing disease, though they call this moral cancer highmindedness? The foundation of this pride is usually high office and the power that goes with it. For they are affected by it either in the office itself, or whilst preparing for it; even talking about it will often fan the latent disease. But what words could penetrate their hearing which is already filled with the voice of the heralds? Who shall convince people in such a frame of mind that they are just like actors parading on the stage? For these, too, don a delicately polished mask and a gold-embroidered purple robe, and proceed solemnly in a chariot. Nevertheless the disease of pride does not invade them on account of this. But their frame of mind remains at the procession the same as it was before they appeared on the stage; and later they are not sorry to have to descend from the chariot and to discard their dignity.

Yet those whose office causes them to parade on the stage of life consider neither the past nor the future, but are blown up by conceit like bubbles. So the loud voice of the herald causes them to swell; they mould themselves another kind of face, changing completely the features of their natural face into something grim and awe-inspiring. They adopt a harsher voice which is transposed into a fiercer key to frighten their hearers. They remain no longer within human limits, but intrude themselves into the authority of Divine power. For they imagine themselves master over life and death, because, having to judge men, they bestow on some the sentence of acquittal, while condemning others to death. And they do not even realize who is the true Master of human life, who determines the beginning as well as the end of existence. Yet this alone should be sufficient to check conceit, to see so many magistrates on the very stage of their office snatched away from their bench and carried out to their graves, where the place of the herald's voice is taken by the dirge.

How then can a man be master of another's life, if he

is not even master of his own? Hence he ought to be poor in spirit, and look at Him who for our sake became poor of His own will; let him consider that we are all equal by nature, and not exalt himself impertinently against his own race on account of that deceptive show of office, but, being truly blessed, he will gain the Kingdom of Heaven in exchange for humility in this transitory life.

Nor should you, my dear brethren, disregard the other interpretation of poverty which begets the riches of Heaven. *Sell*, He says, *all thy possessions and give to the poor, and come follow me, and thou shalt have treasure in Heaven.*[13] It seems to me that this kind of poverty does not differ from the one that is called blessed. *Behold, we have left all we had and followed Thee,* says the disciple to the Master, *what therefore shall we have?* And what is the answer? *Blessed are the poor in spirit, for theirs is the Kingdom of Heaven.*[14] Would you like to know who it is that is poor in spirit? He who is given the riches of the soul in exchange for material wealth, who is poor for the sake of the spirit. He has shaken off earthly riches like a burden so that he may be lightly lifted into the air and be borne upwards, as says the Apostle, *in the cloud walking on high together with God.*[15]

Gold is a heavy thing, and heavy is every kind of matter that is sought after for the sake of wealth—but virtue is light and bears souls upwards. Truly these two, heaviness and lightness, are opposed to each other. Therefore, if a man has attached himself to the heaviness of matter, it is impossible for him to become light. Since, then, we ought to tend to the things above, let us become poor in the things that drag us down, so that we may sojourn in the upper regions. The Psalms show us the way: *He hath distributed, he hath given to the poor, his justice remaineth for ever and ever.*[16] The man who gives to the poor will take his share in Him who became poor for our sake. The Lord became poor, so be not afraid of poverty. But He who became poor for us reigns over all creation. Therefore, if you become poor because He became poor, you will also reign because He is reigning. *Blessed are the poor in spirit, for theirs is the Kingdom of Heaven,* of which may we also be made worthy in Christ Jesus Our Lord, to whom be glory and dominion for ever and ever. Amen.

SERMON 2

Blessed are the meek, for they shall inherit the land.

When one climbs up by a ladder he sets foot on the first step, and from there goes on to the one above. Again the second step carries the climber up to the third, and this to the following, and hence to the next. Thus the person who goes up always ascends from where he is to the step above until he reaches the top of his ascent. Now why do I begin like this? It seems to me that the Beatitudes are arranged in order like so many steps, so as to facilitate the ascent from one to the other. For if a man's mind has ascended to the first Beatitude, he will accept what follows as a necessary result of thought, even though the next clause seems to say something new beyond what had been said in the first.

Now the hearer will perhaps object that in the order of steps it is impossible that the inheritance of the earth should be received after the Kingdom of Heaven. He will say that, if the sermon would follow the nature of things, it would have been more fitting to place the earth before Heaven, because our ascent is from the former to the latter. But if the sermon has given us wings, and we have been placed on the ridge of the heavenly ark, we shall then find the supercelestial earth which is reserved to be the inheritance of those who have led a life of virtue. Therefore the order of the Beatitudes seems not to be violated, if God promises us first Heaven and after that earth.

For whatever belongs to the realm of bodily perception is wholly akin only to itself. Even if it appears to be high in terms of spatial relations, it is yet below the intellectual nature, which thought cannot reach unless reason has first caused it to pass beyond those things that are touched by the senses.

Therefore do not be surprised if the celestial regions are called "earth." For the Word, who came down to us because we were unable to rise up to Him, adapts Himself to the lowliness of our understanding. Therefore He communicates the Divine mysteries by words and names that are intelligible to us and uses such expressions as are within the range of human life and circumstances. Thus, in the preceding promise He called that ineffable beatitude in Heaven a "kingdom." But does He intend this word to indicate such things as earthly kingship entails—diadems, for example, studded with sparkling stones, and embroidered purple robes, whose dazzling colours please delicate eyes? Does He suggest vestibules and curtains, thrones raised on high, rows of bodyguards standing round in orderly array, and whatever else those who would emphasize the importance of power are wont to arrange like a play on the stage of their life? No. But he has used this word for describing the good things of Heaven, because the word "kingdom" is something great and above practically all other things that men desire in life. For if something higher than a kingdom existed among men, He would certainly have used that word to rouse the desire for the ineffable beatitude in the souls of His hearers.

For it was impossible that those good things that are above the sense experience and knowledge of men should be revealed to them by their proper names. *For*, the

Apostle says, *eye hath not seen, nor ear heard, nor hath it entered into the heart of man.*[17] But we learn about the ineffable things according to the lowliness of the nature that is ours, so that the hoped-for beatitude may not altogether escape the grasp of our imagination. Therefore the word "earth," though it comes after that of "heaven," should not draw down your thought to the earth below; but if by the preceding Beatitude the Word has raised your minds to the heavenly hope, you should ask me about that earth which is not the inheritance of all, but only of those whose holy life has rendered them worthy of that promise. I think that the great David, guided by the Spirit, has also foreseen this, for the Divine Scripture declares him to have been meek and long-suffering above all his contemporaries. He grasped by faith the things for which we hope, when he said, *I believe to see the good things of the Lord in the land of the living.*[18] For I do not suppose the prophet called this earth *the land of the living*, seeing that it brings forth only mortal things and again dissolves into itself everything that comes from it. But he meant the land of the living which death does not approach, where they do not tread the way of sinners, and where wickedness finds no foothold. That land, which the sower of tares cannot cut open with his plough of evil, and which therefore does not produce thistles and thorns; but the land of the water of refreshment and the green places, where springs up the fourfold fountain and the vine that is tended by the God of all creation, and all the other things the inspired book teaches us in metaphors.

If we are able to contemplate the transcendent land above the heavens, whose capital is the city of the King, of which, as the prophet says,[19] glorious things are spoken, we shall probably no longer be surprised at the order in which the Beatitudes follow each other. For I do not think this earth here below could reasonably have been offered to the blissful hopes of those who, as the Apostle says, would *be taken up in the clouds to meet the Lord in the air and so be always with the Lord.*[20] Of what use can this earth still be to those whose life is lived in hopes so sublime? For we shall *be taken up in the clouds to meet the Lord in the air, and so be always with the Lord.*

But let us consider the virtue which is meant to be rewarded by the inheritance of the land. He says: *Blessed are the meek, for they shall inherit the land.* What is meekness? And in what respect does the Word call meekness blessed? For if by this expression is meant everything that is done quietly and slowly, I do not think one should indiscriminately consider virtuous whatever is done *in meekness.*[21] For example, among runners the "meek" laggard is not better than the one who races along, nor will a boxer who moves awkwardly take the crown from his opponent. In fact, speaking of our race for the prize of our heavenly vocation, Paul advises us to increase our speed; *So run*, he says, *that you may obtain.*[22] For he himself came to seize what was before him by an increasingly fast movement, forgetting the things he had left behind. He was indeed an agile fighter and watched closely his opponent's assault. Well armed and secure in his step, he did not direct the weapon in his hand against some empty shadow, but he attacked his adversary in his vital parts by inflicting blows on his own body.

Would you like to know Paul's method of fighting? Look at the wounds of his opponent, look at the bruises and marks he left on his defeated enemy. You know very well the adversary who fights through the flesh, and whom he chastizes by his boxing skill.[23] He scratches him with the nails of continence, he mortifies his limbs by hunger and thirst, by cold and nakedness, he inflicts on him the marks of the Lord.[24] He defeats him in the race and leaves him behind, so that no shadow should be thrown across his eyes by the enemy running in front of him. Thus Paul is a swift and nimble fighter, David *enlarges his steps* in pursuit of his enemy,[25] the Bridegroom in the Canticle is likened to a roe because of his speed, *leaping upon the mountains and skipping over the hills;*[26] and there are many other sayings placing speed of movement above the slowness that goes with meekness. Why then does the Word here call meekness a blessed and acceptable quality? For He says: *Blessed are the meek, for they shall inherit the land.* By this He surely means the land that is fruitful in good things, where the tree of life waves its leaves, which is watered by the fountains of spiritual graces. It is the land where sprouts the true vine, and its husbandman, we are told, is the Father of the Lord.[27]

Now what the Word wants to make clear seems something like this. There is a great tendency towards evil in nature, which is quick to turn towards the worse. For example, heavy bodies never move upwards; but if they are flung down from a high mountain ridge, their own weight accelerates the movement, so that they are borne downwards with such force that their speed defies description. Since, therefore, in these circumstances speed is something dangerous, the concept of its opposite would be called blessed. Now the habit that gives way to such downward impulses only slowly and with difficulty is called meekness. For just as fire, whose nature tends always to move upwards, does not move in the opposite direction, so also virtue is quick to tend to the things above without slackening its speed, whereas it is hampered in its movement towards the opposite. Hence, as our nature is very quick to turn towards evil, slowness and quiet in these matters are called blessed. For calm in such things proves the presence of the upward movement.

Perhaps we had better make our meaning clear by an example from life. Everyman is capable of moving his free will in two directions; according to what seems good to him he may be turning towards temperance on the one hand, or towards license on the other. Now what is said to be the form of virtue or vice in a part, is understood to be such also as regards the whole. For man's character is divided into opposite impulses. Wrath is opposed to gentleness, arrogance to modesty; envy to wishing people well, and hate to a loving and peaceable disposition. Human life is, indeed, material, and the passions [28] are concerned with matter; each one of them is possessed by the keen and irrepressible desire for the satisfaction of its will, for matter is heavy and tends downwards. Therefore the Lord calls blessed not those who live in complete isolation from the passions; for it is impossible to secure a perfectly immaterial and passionless mode of life within the confines of a material existence. But He calls meekness a standard of virtue attainable in the life of the flesh, and He says that meekness suffices for beatitude. He does not set up complete absence of passion [29] as a law for human nature; for a just lawgiver could not in fairness command things that nature does not permit. This would be somewhat like making water animals live in the air, or, contrariwise, those that live in the air take to the water. Not so; for a law must be suited to the proper natural capacity.

Hence the Beatitude commands moderation and meekness, but not complete absence of passion; for the latter is outside the scope of nature, whereas the former can be achieved by virtue. If, therefore, the Beatitude ordered man to be unmoved by desires, the blessing would be quite useless for life. Indeed, who could attain to such a state while still united to flesh and blood? But actually He does not say a man is to be condemned if he chances to desire something, but only if of set purpose he lets himself be drawn to passion. For the weakness inherent in our nature frequently causes such desires to arise against our will; it is the work of virtue not to let ourselves be carried away by the impulse of passion as by a torrent, but to resist such leanings manfully and to defeat passion by reason.

Blessed, therefore, are those who are not easily turned towards the passionate movements of the soul, but who are steadied by reason. For the reasoning power restrains the desires like a rein and does not suffer the soul to be carried away to unruliness. How blessed is meekness can best be seen with regard to the passion of wrath. When some word or deed or suspicion causing annoyance has roused this disease, then the blood boils round the heart, and the soul rises up for vengeance. As in pagan fables some drugged drink changes human nature into animal form, so a man is sometimes seen to be changed by wrath into a boar, or dog, or panther, or some other wild animal. His eyes become bloodshot; his hair stands on end and bristles; his voice becomes harsh and his words sharp. His tongue grows numb with passion and refuses to obey the desires of his mind. His lips grow stiff; and unable to articulate a word, they can no longer keep the spittle produced by passion inside the mouth, but dribble froth disgustingly when they try to speak. Hands and feet behave in a similar way, and such is the attitude of the whole body, every limb being affected by this passion.

Though a man might get into such a state—yet if he be guided by the Beatitude, he will appease the disease through reason, cultivating a calm expression and a gentle voice, like a physician who cures the unseemly behaviour of a madman by his art. If you compare the two by contrast, would you not also say that the man who behaves like a brute is pitiable and disgusting, but that the meek man, who does not lose his poise on account of his neighbour's perversity, is to be called blessed?

It is clear that the Word has especially this passion in mind, because He bids us be meek immediately after enjoining humility. For it seems that one closely follows the other, and well-established humility is, as it were, the mother of the habit of meekness. If you free a character from pride, the passion of wrath has no chance of springing up. If men are subject to anger, this disease is caused by insult and dishonour. But insult does not affect a man trained in humility. For if he has purged his mind from human deceit, he will look at the lowliness of the nature allotted to him. He will consider the beginning of his existence as well as the end to which hastens this transitory life. He will realize the filth connected with the flesh and the incompleteness of a nature that is not self-sufficient in regard to its sustenance, but whose deficiency has to be supplied by the abundance of the irrational creatures. He will, moreover, meditate on all the miseries, misfortunes, and manifold forms of disease to which human life is subject, from which no one's nature is altogether immune.

If a man sees these things clearly with the purified eye of the soul, he will not easily be annoyed by the absence of honours. On the contrary, if honour is given to him for some reason or other by his neighbour, he will think it acquired under false pretences, since there is in our nature nothing connected with honour, save only what regards the soul; and its honour does not consist in the things coveted after the manner of this world. For to boast of riches or to be proud of one's family, to have regard to fame and to think oneself above one's neighbour, all these things in which human honour consists are but destruction and shame to the honour of the soul. Therefore no right-thinking man should choose to defile the purity of his soul with such a thing. To be of this mind is precisely to be habitually profoundly humble, for if humility is well-established, wrath will find no entrance into the soul. And if wrath is absent, life will be in a settled state of peace. Now this is nothing else but meekness, the end of which is beatitude and the inheritance of the heavenly country in Christ Jesus, to whom be glory and dominion for ever and ever. Amen.

Blessed are they that mourn, for they shall be comforted.

We have not yet reached the summit of the mountain, but our minds are still at its foot. Even though we have already passed two hills and have been led up by the Beatitudes to blessed poverty and to the meekness that surpasses it, the Word now guides us to yet higher things. In orderly sequence He shows us through the Beatitudes the third height. To this one can ascend only, as the Apostle says, *Laying aside every weight and sin which surround us,*[30] and having thus come to the summit burdenless and light, our souls will approach truth in a purer light.

Now what does this saying mean: *Blessed are they that mourn, for they shall be comforted?* If one looks at it from the point of view of the world, he will certainly say that the words are ridiculous, and argue like this: If one calls blessed those people whose life is spent enduring all manner of misfortune, it follows that those who live without sorrow or care must be miserable. Then he will enumerate the various kinds of calamities and will further provoke laughter among his audience by giving a vivid description of the miseries of widowhood and the sad condition of orphans. He will mention financial losses, shipwrecks, and the fate of prisoners of war; he will proceed to unjust judgements in lawcourts, to exile, confiscation of property, and loss of one's honour. He will enlarge on the calamities resulting from illness, such as blindness, mutilations, and any sort of physical ailment. In short, he will show in detail every kind of suffering, whether of body or soul, that may afflict men in this life. And thus he thinks he will have made appear ridiculous the saying that calls blessed those that mourn.

We, however, care little about those who consider the Divine thoughts in a mean, unworthy spirit, and will try as far as possible to examine the riches that lie hidden in the depth of the saying. Then it will perhaps become clear how very different is the mind that is concerned with the sublime things of Heaven from that which is carnal and clings to the earth.

Now in the first place one can take that mourning to be blessed which follows the transgressions of sinners, according to St. Paul's teaching on sorrow. He says [31] that there is more than one kind of sorrow, the one of the world, the other brought about by God; and that the work of the worldly sorrow is death, whereas the other works in those afflicted with it salvation through repentance. For surely, if a soul bewails its wicked life because it feels its bad effects, such suffering cannot be excluded from the sorrow that is called blessed. It is with this as with physical ailments. If through some accident a part of the body has become paralyzed, insensibility is a sign that the affected limb has gone dead. But if medical skill has restored to the body the sensibility of life, both patient and doctors are glad when the sick part feels pain; for the fact that the limb can already feel what causes pain is a sign that the illness has turned the corner. Thus, as the Apostle says, [32] if people indulge in a life of sin because they no longer feel pain, they have become truly paralyzed and are dead to the life of virtue, for they have no feeling for what they are doing.

But then some healing word may lay hold of them like a bitterly pungent medicine—I speak of the fierce threats of the Judgement to come—and pierce the heart to its depth with the fear of the things that are to be expected. It would tell them of the terror of hell and the unquenchable fire, of the worm that does not die and the gnashing of teeth, the perpetual weeping and the outer darkness.[33] All these things would be rubbed in like pungent medicines, and so the man who had been numbed by the passions and pleasures of the senses would be warmed again and made to realize what kind of life he had been leading, and he would become blessed through the pain he would feel in his soul.

In this way Paul's words chastized the man who had violated his father's marriage bed as long as he remained unconscious of his sin; but when the medicine of correction had struck home, he began to comfort him as if he had already become blessed by his sorrow, *lest,* as he says, *perhaps such a one be swallowed up with overmuch sorsow.*[34] So let us also reflect on this when we consider the Beatitude before us; for this is not without profit even for a virtuous life, seeing that human nature somehow abounds with sin, the remedy of which is shown to be the sorrow of repentance.

But it seems to me that the Word indicates something deeper than what has so far been said, and intends us to understand something else by the steady, invigorating influence of sorrow. For if He meant to indicate only repentance for sin, it would have been more consistent to call blessed those who have mourned rather than those who are always mourning. Taking by way of comparison an example from illness, we would call blessed those who are healed, but not those who are forever in process of being healed. Obviously the continual healing would indicate at the same time the continued existence of the disease.

In another respect, too, I think we ought not to cling to this meaning, as if the Word had assigned this Beatitude only to those mourning for sin. For we shall find many who have led a blameless life, to which this same Divine Voice has borne witness that it was in every way praiseworthy. Thus, was John by any chance covetous? Was Elias an idolater? Which sin, great or small, does history record in the lives of these men? What about it? Is the Word going to exclude them from this Beatitude, because from the very beginning they were not sick nor in need of this remedy—I mean of the sorrow that comes from repentance? Would it not be absurd to suppose these to be excluded from the Divine Beatitude because they neither sinned nor cured sin by sorrow? Would not this mean that it would be better to sin than to live without sin, if the grace of the Comforter [35] were to be given only to those who repent? For He says, *Blessed are they that mourn, for they shall be comforted.* Let us therefore follow as far as possible Him who, as Habacuc says, *leads me upon the high places,* [36] and examine again the meaning contained in the saying, in order to learn to what kind of mourning the comforting of the Holy Spirit is promised.

Hence let us scrutinize the human life to find first what this mourning is in itself, and why it arises. Now it is evident to all that mourning is a sorrowful disposition of the soul which arises from being deprived of some of the things that are pleasant, a sorrow which finds no place in people who spend their life in happiness. Take as an example a man whose life is altogether flourishing. All things go well with him and according to plan. He is happily married, pleased with his children, and can rely on the help of his relatives. He is respected in the community and held in honour by the authorities. His opponents fear him, his subjects esteem him. He is always welcome to his friends, wealthy, enjoying life, pleasant, carefree, and of robust physique. In fact, he has everything the world thinks worthwhile. A man like this thoroughly enjoys all things of this present world. But supposing there was a change in his prosperous circumstances. Perhaps some misfortune caused him to be separated from his dear ones, he might lose his property or suffer in his health. Then the removal of something pleasant would bring about the opposite disposition, and this we call mourning. Therefore the definition we have given is correct, and mourning is a painful sensation caused by the privation of what is pleasant.

If then we understand human sorrow, this sorrow, which is well-known, should be a guide to what is unknown, so that it may become clear what is this mourning that is called blessed, and that is followed by comforting. For though the loss of the good things a man possessed causes sorrow here below, yet no one will grieve for the loss of things unknown to him. Therefore we must first know what really is the true good, and then, with this in mind, consider human nature. For only thus can we attain to the mourning that is called blessed.

Let us take for an example two men living in a dark place, one of whom had been born in the dark, whilst the other had been used to enjoying the light outside and has somehow been shut up in that place by force. Surely the present calamity will not affect both in the same way; for the man who knows of what he has been deprived will think the loss of light a very grave matter, whereas the one who does not know this gift at all will continue to live without sorrow. He will not think that he has lost anything worth having, because he has been brought up in darkness. And so the desire to enjoy the light will induce the one to use every device he can think of in order to see once more what has been taken from him by force, whereas the other man will grow old in darkness; for he will think good what he has because he does not know anything better.

It is the same with the subject of our present meditation. If a man has been able to perceive the true good, and then realizes the poverty of human nature, he will certainly think the soul in distress. For he will consider that the present life is spent in sorrow, because it is removed from this true good. Therefore I would say that the Word does not call blessed the sorrow itself, but rather the realization of the good that produces this state of sorrow, which is due to the fact that the object of the desire is absent from our life.

After this we have to ask what is this light which, in this life, does not shine into this cave of our human nature.[37] Can it be that we desire something vain and elusive? For what human thought can search out the nature of what we seek? What names or expressions can we invent to produce in us a worthy conception of the light beyond? How shall I name the invisible, how describe the immaterial? How shall I show what cannot be seen, or comprehend what has neither size nor quantity, neither quality nor form? How can I grasp what is neither in place nor in time, which eludes all limitation and every form of definition? For His work is life and the substance of all good things, and with Him everything sublime in thought and word is concerned. Whether it be called Godhead, or Kingdom, power, eternity and incorruption, joy or exultation—every noble thought and word is related to Him. By what line of thought can this Divine goodness enter our consciousness, this goodness that can be contemplated yet cannot be seen? Which gives being to all things, but itself is ever-existing and has no need of becoming?

But lest our words should labour in vain in our effort to reach what is inaccessible, we will cut short our enquiry into the nature of the transcendent good; for it is impossible that such a thing should come within the scope of our comprehension. We have, however, gained one advantage from our examination: we have succeeded in forming an idea of the greatness of what we have sought by the very fact of having been unable to perceive it. And the more we believe the nature of the good to exceed our comprehension, the more should our sorrow grow within us, because we are separated from a good so great that we cannot even attain to its knowledge. Yet once we did share in this good that surpasses every power of perception. Indeed our nature shared in this good that transcends all thought to such an extent that the human being seemed to be another such, since it was fashioned to the most exact likeness [38] in the image of its prototype. For all those attributes of His on which we now speculate and conjecture, once also belonged to man, such as incorruptibility and beatitude, the power to govern oneself without a master, and to lead a life devoid of grief and labour. Man then passed his life in Divine things, and contemplated the Good with a pure mind devoid of veils.

The story of the creation of the world hints at all these things in a few words, when it says that man was made in the image of God and lived in Paradise, enjoying the things that were growing there. But the fruit of those plants was life, knowledge, and things like that. If these once belonged to us, how should we not bewail our misfortune, when we contrast our former beatitude with our present misery? What was exalted has been brought low, and what was made in the image of Heaven has been reduced to earth. What was meant to rule has been enslaved, and what had been created for immortality has been destroyed by death. Man, who once lived in the delights of Paradise, has been transplanted into this unhealthy and wearisome place, where his life, once accustomed to impassibility, became instead subject to passion and corruption.

Thus the creature that had once been without a master and in full possession of his free will, is now dominated by so many great evils that we can hardly count all our tyrants. For as soon as any of our innate passions is allowed to dominate, it becomes the master of the person it has enslaved. It occupies the castle of the soul like a tyrant, and afflicts the obedient lord through his own subjects. It uses our thoughts as its servants who carry out what seems good to it. For the whole array of passions, wrath and fear, cowardice and impudence, depression as well as pleasure, hatred, strife and merciless cruelty, envy as well as flattery, brutality together with brooding over injuries—they all are so many despotic masters who make the soul a slave in their territory as if it was a prisoner of war. If one were to add to this also the physical sufferings that are insolubly bound up with our nature, I mean the manifold forms of disease from all of which human nature was originally immune, our tears would flow still more, as we were comparing and contrasting what is painful and evil with the things that were good and pleasant.

Hence, when He calls mourning blessed, the underlying sense seems to be that the soul should turn to the true good and not immerse itself in the deceits of this present life. For no one who has clearly seen these things can live without tears himself, or fail to think miserable any one deeply involved in the pleasures of this life. We can see something similar in the animals. Their natural situation is indeed pitiable; for what is more to be regretted than the lack of reason? Yet they have no sense of their misfortune; on the contrary, their life, too, affords a certain pleasure. The horse prances, the bull kicks up dust, and the boar makes his bristles stand up. The puppies play and the calves leap; in short, in every animal there are certain signs by which they show pleasure. Yet, if they knew anything of the gift of reason, they would not spend their dumb and miserable life in pleasure. It is the same with those men who do not know the good things of which our nature has been deprived, and who therefore spend their present life in the pursuit of pleasure.

It follows from this that people who enjoy the present things do not look for better ones. But if a man does not seek, he will not find what comes only to those who seek. For this reason the Word calls mourning blessed. He does not judge it blessed for its own sake, but because of the results that follow from it. Now the context shows that mourning is something blessed for men because of the reference to consolation. For He says, *Blessed are they that mourn;* however He does not finish the sentence here, but adds, *for they shall be comforted.*

I think the great Moses had already observed this before —or rather the Word, who disposed these things in him— in connection with the mystical observance of the Pasch. For he prescribed unleavened bread during the days of the feast, but for the seasoning of the food he appointed bitter herbs.[39] Thus we were to learn that we can partake of the mystical feast [40] in no other way except by mingling voluntarily the bitter herbs of this earthly life (*bios*) with the simple and unleavened life (*zoe*).[41] The great David saw indeed that he had arrived at the highest peak of good fortune, I mean at kingship. Yet he lavishly adds bitter herbs to his life, sighing and loudly lamenting his continued sojourn in the flesh. He almost faints away with desire for the better things. *Woe is me,* he says, *that my sojourning is prolonged.*[42] Elsewhere [43] he gazes intently at the loveliness of the Divine Tabernacles and says that he faints away with desire, for he prefers being given the last place there to having the first in the present world.

But if one would like to realize even more clearly the power of this blessed mourning, he should examine it for himself in the story of the rich man and Lazarus, where this teaching is explained more lucidly. *Remember,* says Abraham to the rich man, *that thou didst receive good things in thy lifetime, and likewise Lazarus evil things; therefore now he is comforted, and thou art tormented.*[44] For this is right, seeing that want of advice, or rather bad advice, has removed us from the good destiny God had intended for us. God had laid down that we should enjoy the good things unmixed with evil; He had forbidden to join the experience of evil to what was good. Yet through our gluttony we filled ourselves voluntarily with the opposite, I mean we tasted disobedience to the Word of God. Hence human nature must now always live in both, and share in sorrow as well as in joy.

Since then there are two spheres of life, and life is considered in a double way, according to the diversity of these two spheres, thus there is also a twofold joy, the one belonging to this life, the other to the life that is presented to our hope. Therefore we should think it blessed to reserve our share of joy for the truly good things in eternal life, and to fulfil the duty of sorrow in this short and transitory life. We should not think it a loss to be deprived of some of the pleasant things of this life, but rather to lose the better things for the sake of enjoying the others. If therefore it is blissful to have the unending and everlasting joy in eternity, human nature is bound also to taste of the opposite. Then it will no longer be difficult to see the meaning of the passage, why those who mourn now are blessed, because they shall be comforted in the world without end. Now the comfort comes through participating in the Comforter. For the gift of comforting is the special operation of the Spirit, of which may we also be made worthy, through the grace of Our Lord Jesus Christ, to whom be glory for ever and ever. Amen.

SERMON 4

Blessed are they that hunger and thirst after justice, for they shall have their fill.

The medical experts tell us that people who are suffering from loss of appetite always seem to be perfectly satisfied, because certain bad juices and excretions flow together in the upper part of the stomach. Hence they are without desire for wholesome food, since their natural appetite has been destroyed by a spurious satiety. But if some medical treatment is applied and the juices blocking up the cavities of the stomach have been purged by some laxative medicine, the healthy appetite for nourishing food returns, because the natural functions are no longer hindered by foreign matter. It is a sign of health that the patients take food no longer because they are forced to do so, but with desire and relish.

Why do I start with this opening? The Word which proceeds by successive stages leads us by the hand to the higher steps of the ladder of the Beatitudes. As the Prophet says,[45] He has disposed beautiful steps in our heart, and so, after the ascensions that have been accomplished before, He shows us another step: *Blessed are they that hunger and thirst after justice, for they shall have their fill.* I think it is right that after the glutted satiety of the soul has been purged away as much as possible, we should be filled with the blessed desire of such food and drink. For a man cannot be strong unless his vigour is sustained by sufficient food, nor can he take in food without eating, or eat without having an appetite. Strength, then, is one of the good things of life. Now strength is preserved by being sufficiently filled, and this is brought about by food. But eating depends on appetite. Appetite, therefore, should be a blessed thing for living creatures, since it is the principle and cause of our strength. Now as regards material food, we do not all relish the same things; but the desires of men at table vary according to the diversity of foods. One likes sweet things, the other hot and piquant courses; one prefers something salted, the other a sour dish. But it often happens that a person's taste is not for the things that are good for him. If someone's particular constitution has a tendency towards a certain disease, he will cause it to grow by his predilection for the wrong kinds of food. But if he shows an appetite for what is wholesome, he will live in perfect health, because the food makes at the same time for his well-being.

So it is also with the food of the soul. Everyone's desire is not for the same. Some people covet glory, or wealth, or prominence. The desire of others is incessantly occupied with the table. Others again lap up envy like some noxious food; and then there are also some who desire things whose nature is good. Now what is good by nature is the same for all and at all times. It is that which is desirable not because of something else, but for its own sake. It is always the same, and satiety can never blunt its attraction. Therefore the Word calls blessed those who hunger not without qualification, but those whose desire is directed towards true justice.

What then is justice? This, I think, we must first explain in our sermon; for only when its beauty has been shown can the desire for this lovely thing be roused in us. It is impossible to desire something of which one is not aware; our nature is slow to be moved towards what it does not know, unless by hearing or sight it first conceive some idea of the desirable object.

Thinkers who have investigated these matters say that justice is the disposition to distribute equally to each, according to his worth. For example, if someone is charged with distributing money, he will be called just if he aims at equity and fits the gift to the needs of the recipients. Again, a man invested with the authority of a judge will not pass sentence according to favour or disfavour; but he will be guided by the nature of the case and punish those who deserve punishment whilst acquitting the innocent. In other matters of dispute he will give judgement according to truth. Such a man will be called just. It is the same with a person who imposes taxes on his subjects, which he should do in accordance with their capacity. Or take the master of a household, the ruler of a city, or the king of a nation. If any of these men rule his subjects fairly, that is to say, if he does not take advantage of his power to indulge irrational impulses, but judges them squarely, adapting his sentence to their situation, he will come within the definition of those who attribute precisely such conduct to the notion of justice.

But as I look up to the sublime laws of God, I come to realize that one must see something higher in this justice than what has been discussed hitherto. The word of salvation is indeed given as a common good for all mankind, but not every man is concerned with the things that have just been mentioned. For only few are called to reign or govern, to give judgement or to have power of administering money or other revenues; whereas the majority of men are subjects of rulers and administrators. How then can one accept as true justice what is not meant equally for all? For if, according to the words of those outside the fold, the purpose of the just man is equality; but on the other hand pre-eminence presupposes inequality, then this definition of justice cannot be regarded as true, because it is at once completely refuted by the inequality of life.

What then is the justice that belongs to all, and which everyone should desire who belongs to the table of the Gospel? Whether a man be rich or poor, servant or master, whether he be of noble family or a slave, no condition either increases or decreases the quality of justice. For if this were present only in a man of great authority and prominence, how could Lazarus be just? He was cast outside the rich man's gate and had no material, as it were, for such justice. He had neither power nor authority, neither house nor table, nor any other of the things in connection with which such justice is practised in this life. For if justice consisted in ruling, or distributing, or administering anything, anyone without such authority would be quite outside the scope of justice. But how could a man be deemed worthy of the eternal rest who had none of those things which, in the general opinion, are the characteristics of justice? Therefore we must search for that kind of justice the fruition of which is promised to him who desires it. For He says: *Blessed are they that hunger after justice, for they shall their fill.*

We need great discernment concerning the many and varied things that exist for our use, and which human nature is impelled to desire. For we must distinguish the useful from the harmful in these kinds of foods; else what the soul would take for food might bring about our ruin and death instead of life. Therefore it may not be amiss to elucidate the sense of this by some further inquiry into the Gospel.

He who had everything in common with us except sin, and who shared all our sufferings, did not think hunger a sin. Therefore He did not refuse Himself to undergo this experience, but accepted the natural instinct to desire food. Having remained forty days without food, He afterwards was hungry; for when He desired it, He allowed His human nature to act in its normal way. But when the father of temptations realized that He, too, was affected by hunger, he advised Him to meet the desire with stones. Now this means to pervert the desire for natural food into something that is outside nature. He says, *Command that these stones be made bread.*[46]

What is wrong with tilling the land? On what grounds are the seeds rejected and the food they yield despised? Why does he judge the wisdom of the Creator, as if He did not feed mankind properly with grain? Indeed, if stones were more suitable for providing food, then the wisdom of God would have made but poor provision for human life. *Command that these stones be made bread.* Thus he speaks even now to those who are tempted by their own lust, and while saying this he commonly persuades those who pay attention to him to make stones their food. For when desire goes beyond the limits of lawful need, what else is this than the counsel of the devil, who then spurns the food that is made from seeds and incites the appetite to things beyond the limits of nature?

Now people eat food made from stones if their meals betray their avarice, because from their unjust gains they procure for themselves luxurious dishes worth fabulous sums, and the paraphernalia of their dinners are designed only for show so as to impress people, since they far outstrip the necessities of life. For what relation to the needs of nature has this silver which no one can eat and which is displayed in such quantities that it can hardly be carried?

Now what is hunger? Surely the desire for the food one needs. For when the physical vigour is gone, its lack is to be made up again by taking the necessary nourishment. Then nature desires bread, or something else to eat. If, therefore, someone took gold instead of bread into his mouth, would he meet the need? Hence, if a man cares for things he cannot eat instead of for food, he is evidently concerned with stones. While nature seeks one thing, he is busy trying to find another.

Nature says—in fact, by being hungry it almost cries out—that it is now needing food. The strength that has evaporated must be restored to the body. But you do not listen to nature; you do not give it what it is seeking. You think instead of the load of silver you want to be on your table, and so you look for metalworkers. You waste your time on inquiries about images you want carved, so that in these carvings human passions and habits may be reproduced with such technical perfection that you can recognize the wrath of the warrior when he draws his sword for slaughter. You also want to see the pain of the wounded who has received a mortal blow, and whose very appearance seems to wail aloud. You want to look at the attacking hunter as well as at the savage animal, and whatever other things empty-headed people employ artists to execute cleverly in the materials that are used at table.

Nature wants to drink—but you prepare costly tripods,

tankards, mixing bowls, jars, and a thousand other things which have nothing to do with the need in question. Is it not evident that by doing so you listen to him who advises you to pay heed to the stones? But it would be useless to go through the rest of this stony food, the shameless spectacles and the plays that rouse the passions, by which men prepare a way for worse evils to follow, seasoning their food by inciting to licentiousness.

This is the advice the enemy gives in the matter of food; such things he suggests by turning to stones, instead of being content with the ordinary use of bread. But He who overcomes temptation does not eliminate hunger from nature, as if that were a cause of evil. He only removes the worry and fuss which the counsel of the enemy causes to enter together with the need, and leaves nature to adjust itself within its own limits. To give an example: Those who filter the wine do not reject the good liquid on account of the foam mixed up with it; they separate the superfluous matter with a strainer, but do not refuse to use what is pure. The Word acts in the same way. He scrutinizes and distinguishes what is foreign to nature by His subtle and most perfect contemplation. Therefore He does not eliminate hunger, since it is needed to preserve our life; but He does sift out and cast away the superfluous things that have become mixed up with this need, when He says that He knows a bread that nourishes indeed, because the Word of God has adapted it to human nature. If, therefore, Jesus has been hungry, the hunger that is in us as it was in Him should truly be blessed. Hence, if we knew what it was for which the Lord hungered, we should certainly know also the meaning of the Beatitude with which we are now concerned.

What is this food that Jesus is not ashamed to desire? After His conversation with the Samaritan woman He says to His disciples: *My meat is to do the will of the Father.*[48] But the will of the Father is manifest *who will have all men to be saved and to come to the knowledge of the truth.*[49] Now if the Father desires that we should all be saved, and if, therefore, our life is Christ's food, we know how to make use of this hungry condition of the soul. What is this? That we should hunger for our own salvation, that we should thirst for the Divine Will, which is precisely that we should be saved.

So now we have learned from the Beatitude how such a hunger should come to exist in us. For if a man has desired the justice of God, he has found what is truly to be desired. And he satisfies this desire not only in one of the forms this appetite can take; for He wants us to partake of justice not only as food. If the desire took only this form, it would be but half-complete. Now, however, He has disposed that this good thing can also be drunk, so that the intense fervour of the desire should be represented by the passion of thirst. For when we are thirsty we have, as it were, become burning dry, and so approach drink with delight because it will quench this thirst. Though the desire for food and drink is of one kind, yet the form each takes is different. Therefore the Word expresses thus the highest desire for the Good and calls blessed those who suffer both hunger and thirst for justice. For the coveted object is great enough to meet the desire in both ways: grace becomes solid food to the hungry, and drink if a man be drawn to it by thirst.

Blessed are they that hunger and thirst after justice, for they shall have their fill. It may be asked whether it is only blessed to desire justice, whereas if someone had the same longing for temperance or wisdom, prudence or any other kind of virtue, the Word would not call him blessed. But the saying might be interpreted thus: Justice is one of the virtues. Now Divine Scripture frequently expresses the whole by the part, for example, when it gives certain names to the Divine Nature. Thus, speaking in the person of God, the prophecy says: *I the Lord; this is my eternal name, and this is my memorial unto all generations.*[50] And again elsewhere, *I am who am;*[51] and yet in another place, *I am compassionate.*[52] Thus Holy Scripture can call Him by innumerable other names which fittingly signify God's majesty; and so it becomes quite clear to us that when it says one thing the whole series of names is quietly understood to be included as well. For it cannot be supposed that if He is called Lord, He should not also be the other things; but through this one name all others are expressed as well.

So we have learned that the Divinely inspired Word comprehends many things in one part. If, therefore, the Word here calls blessed the hunger of those who desire justice, He includes in this every other form of virtue. Thus a man is equally blessed if he hungers for prudence, or fortitude, or temperance, or anything else that comes under the concept of virtue. For any one form of virtue, divorced from the others, could never by itself be a perfect virtue. For if none of the other good things would appear together with it, their opposites would inevitably find a place in it. Now the opposite of temperance is licentiousness, of prudence folly, and so everything that is accepted as good has something that is known to be its opposite. If, therefore, the other virtues were not all included in justice, it would be impossible that what remained should be good. For no one would say that justice is foolish or rash, licentious or anything else that is known to be evil. But if the conception of justice does not admit of anything bad, it must needs comprise in itself everything good, but what is good belongs to virtue. Therefore every virtue is here comprised under the name of justice. Those who hunger and thirst for it the Word calls blessed and promises them the fulfilment of their desires.

For He says: *Blessed are they that hunger and thirst after justice, for they shall have their fill.* I think the saying means something like this: None of the things that are coveted in this life for the sake of pleasure will satisfy those who run after them, but, as Wisdom says somewhere metaphorically, *A cask full of holes is the occupation with the pleasures of sense.*[53] For those who are always anxiously busy filling it show that their unending labour is fruitless. All the time they are pouring something into the abyss of desire, they add pleasure to pleasure, yet never procure themselves full satisfaction. Who has known avarice come to an end because the man afflicted with it had got what he wanted? Who has ceased to run after fame because he had attained to his heart's desire? But if anyone has indulged to the full what pleases his ears or eyes, his mad craze for the things of the stomach and what comes after the stomach—what has he found to be the result of this enjoyment? Does not every form of pleasure provided by the body vanish almost as soon as it comes, remaining hardly a moment with those who have caught it?

Therefore we learn from the Lord this sublime doctrine that the only truly and solidly existing thing is our zeal for virtue. For if a man has perfected himself in any of the higher things, such as continence, temperance, devotion to God or any other of the sublime teachings of the Gospel, his joy in these achievements does not quickly pass away, but is truly solid, lasting his whole lifetime. Why is this so? Because these things can always be done; there is no moment in the whole of life when we are sick of doing good. For we can always practise temperance and purity, we can be faithful in all that is good and abstain from evil as long as we aim at virtue, and its very practice will bring joy with it. But as for those who waste their lives in absurd lusts, even if their soul should constantly be occupied with licentiousness, yet it will not always be able to enjoy it. For satiety stops the greed of the glutton, and the drinker's pleasure is quenched at the same time as his thirst. And so it is with the other things. They all require a certain interval of time to rekindle the desire for the delights, which enjoyment carried to satiety has caused to flag. The possession of virtue, on the other hand, where it is once firmly established, is neither circumscribed by time nor limited by satiety. On the contrary, it always offers its disciples the ever-fresh experience of the fulness of its own delights. Therefore God the Word promises to those who hunger for these things that they shall be filled, and in being filled their desire will not be dulled but rather kindled anew.

This, then, He teaches us in the discourse from the high mountain of thought: not to desire eagerly any of those things that end in nothingness for those who pursue them. To occupy oneself with them is as devoid of sense as to run after the top of one's own shadow. For such people run on forever, since the object of their pursuit always quickly eludes the pursuer. But we should turn our desire to those things where, if a man exerts himself, the object of his efforts becomes his possession. If a man desires virtue, he makes goodness his very own, for he sees in himself what he has desired. Blessed, therefore, is he who hungers after temperance, for he shall be filled with purity. As has been said, being filled in this way brings about not an aversion, but an intensified desire; both mutually increase each other. The desire of virtue is followed by the possession of what is desired; and the interior goodness brings at the same time unceasing joy to the soul. For such is the nature of this wonderful thing that it not only delights at the moment while one is enjoying it, but brings actual happiness at every instant of time. For if a man has lived rightly, he finds joy in the memory of the past as well as in the virtuous conduct of the present and the expectation of the future reward. This, I suppose, is none other than again virtue itself, which is both the work and the reward of those who have accomplished it.

If we would venture on a bolder interpretation, it seems to me that through the ideas of virtue and justice the Lord proposes Himself to the desire of His hearers. For He became for us wisdom from God, justification, sanctification and redemption, but also Bread descending from Heaven and living water. Somewhere in the Psalms David confesses his thirst for this when he offers this blessed malady to God and says: *My soul hath thirsted after the strong living God. When shall I come and appear before the face of God?* [54] It seems to me that the power of the Spirit has instructed him beforehand in these lofty teachings of the Lord, since he said also that his desire would be fulfilled. *I will appear before Thy sight in justice,* he says, *I shall be satisfied when Thy glory shall appear.* [55] Now in my view this glory is the true virtue, the good that is unmixed with evil, which comprises every concept concerned with goodness. This is God the Word Himself, the virtue that covered the heavens, as Habacuc explains,[56] and rightly have those who hunger for this justice of God been called blessed. For if, as the Psalmist says,[57] a man has truly tasted the Lord; that is, if he has received God into himself, he is filled with Him for whom he has thirsted and hungered, as He has promised who said: *I and my Father will come and will make our abode with him* [58] (the Holy Spirit of course had already been dwelling there before). I suppose the great Paul, too, who had tasted of those ineffable fruits from Paradise, was at the same time full of what he had tasted and always hungering for it. For he owns that he has been filled with what he desired when he says, *Christ liveth in me;* [59] yet he is still hungry, for he always stretches forth to the things before him,[60] saying: *Not as though I had already attained, or were already perfect; but I run that I may apprehend.*[61]

Now may I be allowed to adduce an hypothetical example of something not to be found in nature. Supposing that nothing of the material food that is taken for nourishment were eliminated, but that all were retained in order to add to the stature of the body. Then the bodies would grow to great height, since the daily food would by itself augment their stature. It is the same with justice and every other virtue that goes with it. If, what is eaten in the way of spiritual food be not ejected, it will by constant additions continually increase the stature of those partaking of it. If, therefore, we have understood this blessed hunger, and vomited forth the abundance of evil, let us hunger for the justice of God, that we may be filled with it, in Christ Jesus Our Lord, to whom be glory for ever and ever. Amen.

SERMON 5

Blessed are the merciful, for they shall obtain mercy.

Perhaps this might be compared with the symbolic vision by which Jacob was taught, who saw a ladder stretching from earth to the heights of heaven, and God standing on it.[62]   In the same way we are now taught by the Beatitudes, which elevate those who ascend them to ever higher perceptions.   For I suppose that what was represented to the Patriarch under the form of a ladder was the life of virtue, so that he might learn himself, and teach his posterity, that one cannot be raised to God except by always tending to the things above.   We need an unceasing desire for higher things, which is not content to acquiesce in past achievements; we ought to count it a loss if we fail to progress further.   Now here the sublime teaching of the Beatitudes, which support each other, prepares us to approach God Himself, who is truly blessed and the very ground of all Beatitude.   Therefore, as we approach the wise through wisdom and the pure through purity, so we are also made the friend of the Blessed One through the blessings of the Beatitudes.   For Beatitude is the property of God *par excellence*.   Therefore Jacob tells us that God was leaning on a ladder.   Hence participation in the Beatitudes means nothing else but to have communion with the Godhead, to which the Lord raises us by His sayings.

So it seems to me that, through the effect that follows

the Beatitude under consideration, He divinizes,[63] as it were, His hearer, if he understands the word rightly. For He says: *Blessed are the merciful, for they shall obtain mercy.* Now I know that in many passages of the Divine Scripture holy men call the Divine Power merciful; as does David in the Psalms, Jonas in his prophecy, and the great Moses frequently in the Law. If, therefore, the term "merciful" is suited to God, what else does the Word invite you to become but God, since you ought to model yourself on the property of the Godhead? For if the Divinely inspired Scripture calls God merciful, and if the Divinity is truly blessed, then it should be clear how the following is to be understood. It means that if a man is merciful, he is deemed worthy of the Divine Beatitude, because he has attained to that which characterizes the Divine Nature. *The Lord is merciful and just, and our God showeth mercy.*[64] How, therefore, could a man be other than blessed who both is called and actually is the same as that for which God is named blessed because He does it? Now the holy Apostle counsels us in one of his letters to *be zealous for the better gifts.*[65] It is our aim not that we should be persuaded to desire the things that are good; (for to incline towards the good is one of the inherent characteristics of human nature)—but that we should not be mistaken in our judgement as to what is good. It is here that our life is most subject to error, that we cannot clearly distinguish what is good by nature and what is mistakenly supposed to be such. For if evil was presented to our life in its nakedness, unadorned with some semblance of good, mankind would surely not fly to it so easily. Therefore we need prudence in order to understand the passage we are considering, so that we may first learn what is the true beauty it contains, and then conform ourselves to it.

The conception of the Divine is by nature inherent in all men; but ignorance of the true God is responsible for the gross errors in regard to the object of worship. Some indeed venerate the true Godhead which is contemplated in the Father, the Son, and the Holy Spirit; but others have been led astray to absurd ideas by supposing this to be in a creature; and by thus swerving a little from the truth, they have opened the door to impiety. So it is also in the thought we are considering: if we do not apprehend its real meaning, the result for us will be a considerable loss of truth.

Now what is mercy, and in regard to what is it practised? And how is he blessed to whom is returned what he gives? For He says, *Blessed are the merciful, for they shall obtain mercy.* The obvious meaning of the words calls men to mutual charity and sympathy, which are demanded by the capricious inequality of the circumstances of life; for all live not in the same conditions, neither as regards reputation nor physical constitution nor other assets. Life is in many ways divided up into opposites, since it may be spent as slave or as master, in riches or poverty, in fame or dishonour, in bodily infirmity or in good health—in all such things there is division. Therefore the creature in need should be made equal to the one who has a larger share, and that which goes short should be filled by what has abundance; this is the law mercy gives men in regard to the needy. For unless mercy soften the soul, man cannot arrive at healing the ills of his neighbour, since mercy is defined as the opposite of cruelty. The hard and cruel man is inaccessible to those who would approach him; whereas the merciful person is, as it were, predisposed by his attitude to give the sympathy that is needed, so that he can become to the afflicted exactly what the distressed mind is looking for. To sum up the explanation in a definition: Mercy is a voluntary sorrow that joins itself to the sufferings of others.

However, if we should not yet have made its meaning clear, perhaps it may be explained more lucidly by another definition. Mercy is the loving disposition towards those who suffer distress. For as unkindness and cruelty have their origin in hate, so mercy springs from love, without which it could not exist. And if one would carefully go into the distinctive property of mercy, he would find it in an intensely loving disposition combined with the affect of sorrow. For all, friends and foes alike, seek a share in a man's good luck; whereas it is a sign of those ruled by charity to want a share also in his misfortunes. Charity, on the other hand, is admittedly more excellent than anything else that is pursued in this life. Now mercy is intensified charity. Hence a man of such disposition of soul is truly blessed, since he has reached the summit of virtue.

Let no one think that this virtue is concerned only with material things; else it could be attained only by someone who has the necessary means for doing good. No; it seems to me more adequate to place such a virtue in the choice of the will. For if a man only wills the good, but is prevented from accomplishing it by lack of means, he is not inferior, as regards his state of soul, to the person who shows his intention by works. Therefore we need not explain in detail how much we gain for our life if we understand the meaning of the Beatitude in this way; even to the quite simple the advantages this counsel has for our life should be perfectly clear. If, by hypothesis, such attitude of mind to our inferiors were innate in all of us, there would no longer be either superfluity or want. Life would no longer be lived in diametrically opposite ways; man would no longer be distressed by want or humiliated by slavery, nor would dishonour sadden him. For all things would be common to all, and his life as a citizen would be marked by complete equality before the law, since the man who was responsible for the government would of his own free will be on a level with the rest.

If such a state of affairs could become a fact, no cause would be left for enmity. Envy would be futile, hate would die out, remembrance of injuries would be banished along with lies, fraud, and war, all of which are the offspring of covetousness. If that hard and unfeeling attitude were removed, the evil growths would be weeded out with it completely, as with the root of wickedness. And with the departure of evils there would enter instead the whole array of good things, peace and justice with all their train of virtues. What could be thought to be more blessed than to live thus, when we would no longer have to entrust the safety of our lives to bolts and stones, but were secure in each other's keeping? For just as the harsh and cruel man makes enemies of those who have come to experience his savagery; so also, contrariwise, we become all friendly with the merciful man, since mercy naturally engenders love in those who share in it. Therefore mercy, as the definition has shown, is the parent of kindness, and the pledge of charity; it is the bond of all loving disposition. How could one imagine a more stable security for life than this? Rightly, therefore, does the Word call the merciful blessed, since this name comprises so many wonderful things.

However, everyone knows that this counsel is profitable for our life. Yet I think that, by the choice of the future tense, the passage secretly suggests something more than is perceived at first sight. He says, *Blessed are the merciful, for they shall obtain mercy*, implying that the merciful will have their reward reserved for later.

Therefore we would disregard the obvious meaning as far as we can, since it is easily understood and quickly discovered by everybody; but we will endeavour as much as possible to let our mind penetrate the interior of the veil. *Blessed are the merciful, for they shall obtain mercy.* From this passage a higher doctrine may be learned. It is this. He who made man in His own image endowed the nature of His handiwork with the principles of all goodness. Hence nothing good enters into us from outside, but it lies with us to have what we will, and to bring forth the good from our nature as if from some inner chamber. For from the parts we are taught about the whole, that there is no other way of obtaining one's desire except by procuring the good for oneself. Therefore the Lord says to His hearers: *The Kingdom of God is within you;* [66] and, *Everyone that asketh receiveth; and he that seeketh findeth; and to him that knocketh, it shall be opened.* [67] So it depends on us and is in the power of our free will to receive what we desire, to find what we seek, and to enter where we wish to be. Consequently the opposite is equally affirmed together with this, namely, that the inclination towards evil also comes into existence uncompelled by any external necessity. Evil subsists as soon as it is chosen; it comes into being whenever we elect it. It has no substance of its own; apart from deliberate choice evil exists nowhere.[68]

Hence it is evident that the Lord of nature has endowed the nature of man with the power of ruling itself and willing freely. For all things, whether good or bad, depend on our choice. But the incorruptible and just sentence of the Divine Judgement follows the choice we have made according to our purpose, and distributes to each what he has happened to prepare for himself. *To them indeed,* as says the Apostle, *who, according to patience, in good work, seek glory and honour . . . eternal life; but to them that . . . obey not the truth but give credit to iniquity, wrath and indignation,*[69] and whatever other words signify the bitter retribution. For mirrors [70] show the faces they reflect precisely as they are, cheerful of those who are cheerful, gloomy of those who look sad. Yet no one would hold the nature of the mirror responsible for the gloom of the face reflected, if the original itself shows depression. So also God's just Judgement adapts itself to our own dispositions; according as we do, it provides for us from our own.

Come, He says, *ye blessed,* and, *Depart, you cursed.*[71] Is there any external necessity here why those on the right should be addressed with the sweet, those on the left with the bitter words? Have not the former received mercy through what they have done, and the latter made God cruel to themselves because they behaved cruelly to their own kind? This rich man who frittered away his life in luxuries has not shown mercy to the poor in distress before his gate, wherefore he has cut himself off from mercy, and when he asks for mercy, he is not heard; not because one drop would have diminished the great fountain of Paradise, but because the drop of mercy cannot mix with cruelty. *For what fellowship has light with darkness?* [72] *For,* He says, *what things a man shall sow, those also shall he reap. For he that soweth in his flesh, of the flesh also shall reap corruption. But he that soweth in the spirit, of the spirit shall reap life everlasting.* [73] The seed I take to be a man's own choice, the harvest the retribution which follows that choice. To those who have chosen good things the ear of corn will yield the same; whereas those who have cast thorny seeds in their life, will laboriously gather the thorns. For a man must needs reap the same as he has sown, it cannot be otherwise.

Blessed are the merciful, for they shall obtain mercy. Which human reason could plumb the depth of thought contained in these words? The fact that this saying is quite without qualifications induces us to go more carefully into what has been said. For He added no indication as to who the people are to whom one ought to show mercy, but He says simply, *Blessed are the merciful.* Perhaps, taking into account what has already been said, the Word suggests to us somehow that the idea of mercy follows from the sorrow that is called blessed. There a man who spends his life in sorrow was pronounced blessed, and here, I think, the Word inculcates the same teaching. For we are affected by the ills of others, when our friends have met with grievous misfortunes. They may, for example, have been driven from their father's house, have escaped with their bare life from shipwreck, or come into the power of pirates or robbers. They may have been made slaves from freemen, or from happy circumstances have been reduced to the state of captives. Briefly, they were once held to be favoured by fortune, but have now met with some such adversity. On account of these things our souls would be inclined to sorrow. But perhaps it would be much more appropriate if we were so disposed with regard to ourselves, on account of the wound that has been inflicted on our life contrary to its original dignity. We need only consider the glorious home from which we have been driven out, how we have fallen among the robbers, and, defenceless and naked, were left submerged in the depths of this life. We need but reflect on the nature and number of those great tyrants into whose service we have been pressed instead of leading a free and independent life, and how we have spoiled this life of bliss by death and corruption.

How is it possible that with this in mind we should spend our pity on the misfortunes of others? Should the soul not rather be disposed to have pity on itself if it thinks of what it once possessed, and from what state it has fallen? For what is more pitiable than this captivity? Instead of enjoying Paradise, we have been allotted this unwholesome place where to live and toil; instead of being impassible, we have been doomed to passions without number. Instead of living with the angels on the heights, we have been condemned to dwell with the beasts of the earth. Yes, we have exchanged an angelic existence free from passions for the life of the brutes—and who could easily tell the number of stern masters to whose rage our life is now subject? Wrath is a bitter despot, and so is envy. Hate and the vice of pride are raging tyrants, thoughts of license behave insolently as if dealing with slaves and bring nature into bondage to passions and impurity; but greed greatly surpasses all other tyranny in venom. For it enslaves the miserable soul and compels it always to fulfil its insatiable desires; it is constantly filled, yet never satisfied. It is like a many-headed monster which, through innumerable mouths, provides food for a stomach that is never filled. It has never gained enough, but whatever it receives becomes invariably fuel kindling the desire for more. Hence, if one considers this wretched life, how could he be altogether without pity for such calamities?

The fact that we do not take pity on ourselves is due to our insensibility in the face of these evils. It may be compared to the experience of the insane, whom the violence of the disease prevents also from being sensible to what they suffer. If therefore a man knew himself, both what he had once been and what he now is—for Solomon says somewhere that the wise men know themselves—he would never cease to have pity; and this habit of soul would surely be followed by the Divine pity. Therefore He says, *Blessed are the merciful, for they shall obtain mercy.*

They themselves, that is, not others. This is made clear by the words, just as if one said: it is blessed to be concerned with one's physical health. For if a man is concerned about this, he will live in good health. Thus also is the merciful called blessed, because the fruit of mercy becomes itself the possession of the merciful; whether in the sense we have just discovered, or in the one that has been dealt with before; I mean the one that is concerned with the soul's sympathy for the misfortunes of others. Either is equally good, to have pity on oneself in the manner aforesaid, and to sympathize with the misfortunes of our neighbours. For the just judgement of God invests man's goodwill towards the needy with the highest au-

thority; so that in some way man is his own judge, because
he passes sentence on himself by judging those subject to
him.[74]

Now it is believed, and rightly so, that all mankind will
be presented before the judgement seat of Christ, so that
each may receive the things according as he has done in
the body, whether good or bad. Therefore I may perhaps
say something bold: If what is ineffable and invisible be
capable of being apprehended by thought, then one can
even now perceive the blessed reward of the merciful.
For the gratitude of souls who have received kindness towards those who have shown them mercy surely remains
beyond this life in life eternal. What then is likely to
happen in the hour of reckoning, when those who have
received kindness will recognize their benefactor? What
will his soul feel when grateful voices joyfully acclaim him
before the God of all creation? Will he need any other
beatitude added, who in so great a theatre is applauded for
all that is best? For the Word of the Gospel teaches that
those who have received benefits will be present [75] at the
King's Judgement on the just and on sinners. He shows
it to both, pointing as it were with a finger at the things
above—*As long as you did it to one of these my least
brethren.*[76]   By saying *these* He indicates the presence of
those to whom good has been done.

Now if anyone prefers the dead matter of property to
the future beatitude, let him tell me: what is this shining
gold, these glittering jewels, these rich clothes—what kind
of good can he hope these will be? When the King of
creation shall reveal Himself to mankind, seated in splendour on the throne on high, we shall see around Him the
innumerable myriads of angels, and the eyes of all will

perceive the transcendent Kingdom of Heaven. On the other hand, fearful punishments will be revealed; but between these there will be all mankind, all that have existed from the first creation even unto the consummation of the world. And they will stand suspended between fear and hope of the things to come, often trembling, which of the two things that are to be expected will be their final lot. What hope, I say, will he have, when even those who have lived with a good conscience will begin to doubt, as they see others dragged down into that black darkness by their evil conscience as by an executioner. When this man will be led to the Judge accompanied by praise and gratitude from the voices of those to whom he has done good, shining with confidence because of his good works—will he then think material wealth could be compared with this bliss? If all mountains and plains, woods and waters were changed into gold for him, would he accept them in exchange for those marvellous things?

But now consider the man who has carefully shut away his mammon behind seals and bolts and iron-bound doors, in secure hiding places, who has thought the secret accumulation of wealth preferable to any commandment. When, head foremost, he is dragged down into the fire of darkness, all who have experienced it in this life will tax him with his inhuman cruelty. They will say, *Remember that thou didst receive good things in thy lifetime.*[77] You have shut up in the safes mercy along with your riches. You have relinquished mercy on earth; you have not brought neighbourly love to the life here. You do not now have what has never been yours; you do not find what you did not put by. You do not gather what you did not scatter, you do not reap from seeds you did not sow. Your harvest is worthy of your sowing. You have sown bitterness, cull now its sheaves; you have held in esteem the lack of mercy, have now what you have loved. You have looked on no one with sympathy, neither are you now regarded with compassion. You have neglected the afflicted, you shall be neglected when you perish. You have shunned mercy; mercy will shun you. You have abhorred the poor, He who has been poor for your sake will abhor you.

When things such as these shall be said, where will be the gold? Where the splendid vessels? Where will be the security affixed to the treasures by seals? Where will be the dogs that were assigned to watch by night, where the store of arms laid up against burglars? Where will be the accounts entered into the books? What is all this against the weeping and gnashing of teeth? Who will lighten the darkness and extinguish the flame? Who shall turn away the undying worm?

Therefore, brethren, let us heed the voice of the Lord, who in a few words teaches us so many things about the future life. Let us become merciful, so that through mercy we may become blessed, in Christ Jesus Our Lord to whom be glory and power for ever and ever. Amen.

SERMON 6

Blessed are the clean of heart, for they shall see God.

When from the sublime words of the Lord resembling
the summit of a mountain I looked down into the ineffable
depths of His thoughts, my mind had the experience of a
man who gazes from a high ridge into the immense sea
below him. On the coast one can often see some mountain whose front, facing the sea, is cut off straight from
top to bottom, while its projecting upper part forms a
peak overhanging the depth. Now if a man looked down
from such a high peak into the sea below, he would feel
giddy. So also my soul does now, as it is raised from the
ground by this great word of the Lord, *Blessed are the
clean of heart, for they shall see God.* God is promised
to the vision of those whose heart has been purified. But
No man hath seen God at any time,[78] as says the great
John. And the sublime mind of Paul confirms this verdict
when he says, *Whom no man hath seen, nor can see.*[79]
This is the slippery, steep rock that affords no basis for
our thoughts, which the teaching of Moses, too, declared
to be so inaccessible that our mind can nowhere approach
Him. For all possibility of apprehension is taken away by
this explicit denial, *No man can see the Lord and live.*[80]
Yet to see the Lord is eternal life. On the other hand,
those pillars of the faith, John and Paul and Moses, declare
it to be impossible. Do you realize the vertigo of the soul
that is drawn to the depths contemplated in these words?
If God is life, then the man who does not see Him does

not see life. On the other hand, the Divinely inspired prophets and apostles testify that God cannot be seen. Is not the hope of man annihilated? Yet the Lord supports this faltering hope, as He did with Peter whom He put back on the water He had made solid, when he was in danger of sinking. If, therefore, the Hand of the Word is stretched out also to us and confirms in a different view those who have lost their balance in the depths of their speculations, we may be without fear, as we are firmly held by the guiding Hand of the Word. For He says, *Blessed are the clean of heart, for they shall see God.*

Now this promise is so great that it transcends the utmost limits of beatitude. For what else could one desire after such a good, since he possesses all things in the One he contemplates? For according to Scriptural use to see means the same as to have; for example, *Mayst thou see the good things of Jerusalem* [81] instead of "Mayst thou find," which is the meaning of the passage; and *Let the ungodly be taken away, that he may not see the glory of the Lord,* [82] where by not seeing the prophet indicates not participating in. Hence the man who sees God possesses in this act of seeing all there is of the things that are good. By this we understand life without end, eternal incorruption, undying beatitude. With these we shall enjoy the everlasting Kingdom of unceasing happiness; we shall see the true Light and hear the sweet voice of the Spirit; we shall exult perpetually in all that is good in the inaccessible glory.

So magnificent a consummation is offered to our hope in the promise made in the Beatitude. But since, as has been shown before, the seeing has been made dependent on purity of heart, my mind once more grows dizzy, lest perhaps purity of heart should be impossible to achieve because it surpasses our nature. For if the vision of God depends on this; but if, on the other hand, Moses and Paul did not see Him—and it is stated that neither he nor anyone else can see Him [83]—the Word now seems to propose something impossible in the Beatitude. What, therefore, do we gain from knowing how one sees God, if the mind finds it impossible to do so? It would be just as if one said that it is blessed to be in Heaven, because there one contemplates what cannot be seen in this life. Now if this statement also showed a means of journeying to Heaven, it would indeed be profitable to the hearers to learn that it is blessed to be there. But as long as the ascent is impossible, what use is it to know about the Heavenly beatitude? It only saddens those who have learned about it to realize of what things we are deprived, because the ascent is not feasible.

Yet should the Lord command something so great that it completely surpasses our nature and the limits of its power? Surely not. He does not tell those He has not provided with wings to become birds, nor does He bid creatures He has destined to sojourn on land to live in the water. The law is adapted to the capacities of those that receive it in everything else, and nothing is enforced that is beyond nature. Hence we shall realize that neither does the Beatitude set forth what outstrips hope. Nor have John, Paul, Moses, and others like them been lacking in this transcendent beatitude that consists in seeing God. No; for the one said: *There is laid up for me a crown of justice, which the Lord the just Judge will render to me;* [84] the other lay upon the breast of Jesus; [84a] and the third heard the Divine Voice say, *I have known thee above all.* [85]

Now it cannot be doubted that those who have proclaimed the perception of God to be above human power are themselves blessed. On the other hand, beatitude consists in seeing God, and this depends on being pure of heart. Hence surely the purity of heart through which we may become blessed cannot be impossible. How is it then that the voice of the Lord, which promises that God may be seen if we are pure, should not contradict those who, according to St. Paul, evidently speak the truth if they contend that the contemplation of God is beyond our power?

I think it will be best first to say a few words relevant to this subject by way of digression, so that our consideration of the present question may become more methodical. The Divine Nature, whatever It may be in Itself, surpasses every mental concept. For It is altogether inaccessible to reasoning and conjecture, nor has there been found any human faculty capable of perceiving the incomprehensible; for we cannot devise a means of understanding inconceivable things. Therefore the great Apostle calls His ways *unsearchable*,[86] meaning by this that the way that leads to the knowledge of the Divine Essence is inaccessible to thought. That is to say, none of those who have passed through life before us has made known to the intelligence so much as a trace by which might be known what is above knowledge.

Since such is He whose nature is above every nature, the Invisible and Incomprehensible is seen and apprehended in another manner. Many are the modes of such perception. For it is possible to see Him who has *made all things in wisdom*[87] by way of inference through the wisdom that appears in the universe. It is the same as with human works of art where, in a way, the mind can perceive the maker of the product that is before it, because he has left on his work the stamp of his art. In this, however, is seen not the nature of the artist, but only his artistic skill which he has left impressed on his handiwork. Thus also, when we look at the order of creation, we form in our mind an image not of the essence, but of the wisdom of Him who has made all things wisely. And if we consider the cause of our life, that He came to create man not from necessity, but from the free decision of His Goodness, we say that we have contemplated God by this way, that we have apprehended His Goodness—though again not His Essence, but His Goodness. It is the same with all other things that raise the mind to transcendent Goodness, all these we can term apprehensions of God, since each one of these sublime meditations places God within our sight. For power, purity, constancy, freedom from contrariety—all these engrave on the soul the impress of a Divine and transcendent Mind. Hence it is clear through what has just been said that the Lord speaks the truth when He promises that God will be seen by those who have a pure heart; nor does Paul deceive when he asserts in his letters that no one has seen God nor can see Him. For He is invisible by nature, but becomes visible in His energies,[88] for He may be contemplated in the things that are referred to Him.

But the meaning of the Beatitude is not only restricted to this that He who operates can be known by analogy through His operations; for perhaps the wise of this world, too, might gain some knowledge of the transcendent Wisdom and Power from the harmony of the universe. No; I think this magnificent Beatitude proffers another counsel to those able to receive and contemplate what they desire. I make clear by examples what I have in mind.

Bodily health is one of the desirable things in human life; but it is blessed not only to know the principle of health, but to be healthy. For supposing someone had sung the praises of health, yet took some unwholesome food that generated bad juices—what use is it to him to have praised health, seeing he is afflicted with diseases? In the same way, therefore, we should understand the words we are considering. The Lord does not say it is blessed to know something about God, but to have God present within oneself. *Blessed are the clean of heart, for they shall see God.* I do not think that if the eye of one's soul [89] has been purified, he is promised a direct vision of God; but perhaps this marvellous saying may suggest what the Word expresses more clearly when He says to others, *The Kingdom of God is within you.* [90] By this we should learn that if a man's heart has been purified from every creature and all unruly affections, he will see the Image of the Divine Nature in his own beauty. I think that in this short saying the Word expresses some such counsel as this: There is in you, human beings, a desire to contemplate the true good. But when you hear that the Divine Majesty is exalted above the heavens, that Its glory is inexpressible, Its beauty ineffable, and Its Nature inaccessible, do not despair of ever beholding what you desire. It is indeed within your reach; you have within yourselves the standard by which to apprehend the Divine. For He who made you did at the same time endow your nature with this wonderful quality. For God imprinted on it the likeness of the glories of His own Nature, as if moulding the form of a carving into wax. But the evil that has been

poured all around the nature bearing the Divine Image
has rendered useless to you this wonderful thing, that lies
hidden under vile coverings. If, therefore, you wash off
by a good life the filth that has been stuck on your heart
like plaster, the Divine Beauty will again shine forth in
you.

It is the same as happens in the case of iron. If freed
from rust by a whetstone, that which but a moment ago
was black will shine and glisten brightly in the sun. So
it is also with the inner man, which the Lord calls the
heart. When he has scraped off the rustlike dirt which
dank decay has caused to appear on his form, he will once
more recover the likeness of the archetype and be good.
For what is like to the Good is certainly itself good.
Hence, if a man who is pure of heart sees himself, he sees
in himself what he desires; and thus he becomes blessed,
because when he looks at his own purity, he sees the archetype in the image.

To give an example. Though men who see the sun in
a mirror [91] do not gaze at the sky itself, yet they see the sun
in the reflexion of the mirror no less than those who look
at its very orb. So, He says, it is also with you. Even
though you are too weak to perceive the Light Itself, yet,
if you but return to the grace of the Image with which you
were informed from the beginning, you will have all you
seek in yourselves. For the Godhead is purity, freedom
from passion, and separation from all evil. If therefore
these things be in you, God is indeed in you. Hence, if
your thought is without any alloy of evil, free from passion, and alien from all stain, you are blessed because you
are clear of sight. You are able to perceive what is invisible to those who are not purified, because you have been

cleansed; the darkness caused by material entanglements has been removed from the eyes of your soul, and so you see the blessed vision radiant in the pure heaven of your heart. But what is this vision? It is purity, sanctity, simplicity, and other such luminous reflections of the Divine Nature, in which God is contemplated.

Now after what has been said, we do not doubt that such is the case. Yet our sermon is still left with the same impasse which has disconcerted us in the beginning. It is this, that admittedly if someone is in Heaven he shares in the Heavenly marvels; but that the manner of ascent is impossible; and none of the things upon which we have agreed leads us any further. For no one doubts that a man becomes blessed if his heart is purified; but how anyone should cleanse it from its stains, this is what seems to oppose itself to the ascent to Heaven. What then is this Jacob's ladder? How can we find such a fiery chariot by which the prophet Elias was carried up to Heaven, and by which our heart, too, could be lifted up towards the marvels that are above, and shake off this earthly heaviness?

If one considers the inevitable experiences affecting the soul, he will think it absurd and impossible that the evils connected with them should be removed. Our very birth has its beginning in passion, growth proceeds by way of passion, and in passion life also ends. Somehow evil is mixed up with our nature through those who first succumbed to passion, and by their transgerssion made a permanent place for the disease. Now the nature of living beings is transmitted in each species by its descendants so that, according to the law of nature, that which is born is the same as that from which it is born. So man is born from man, the subject of passion from that which is subject to passion, the sinner from the sinner. Hence sin in some way comes into existence together with those who are born; it is born and grows with them, and at the end of life it also ceases with them. Virtue, on the other hand, is hard for us to attain; even with much sweat and pain, zeal and fatigue, one can hardly establish it. This we are taught in many passages of the Divine Scriptures, when we are told that the way of the Kingdom is strait and passes through narrow paths, whereas the way that leads through a life of wickedness to perdition is broad and runs downhill with ease. Yet Scripture affirms that the higher life is not altogether impossible, for the sacred books tell of the wonderful achievements of so many holy men. But since the promise of seeing God has a twofold meaning, on the one hand, that of knowing the Nature that is above the universe, on the other, that of being united to Him through purity of life, we must say that the voice of the Saints declares the former mode of contemplation to be impossible, whereas the second is promised to human nature in Our Lord's present teaching, *Blessed are the clean of heart, for they shall see God.*

Now how you can become pure, you may learn through almost the whole teaching of the Gospel. You need only peruse the precepts one by one to find clearly what it is that purifies the heart. For one can divide wickedness under two headings, the one connected with works, the other with thoughts. The former, that is to say, the iniquity that shows itself in works, He has punished through the Old Law. Now, however, He has given the Law regarding the other form of sin, which punishes not so much the evil deed itself, as guards against even the beginning of it. For to remove evil from the very choice of the will is to free life perfectly from bad works. Since evil has many parts and forms, He has opposed by His precepts its own remedy to each of the forbidden things. The disease of wrath is present everywhere all through life, so He begins the cure from what is most prominent, and first lays down the law to refrain from anger. *You have learned*, He says, from the Old Law, *Thou shalt not kill*.[92] Learn now to keep your soul from wrath against your neighbour. He has not forbidden wrath completely. For sometimes one may lawfully turn such an emotion also to good use; what the precept abolishes is to be angry with one's brother for no good reason—*for everyone who is angry with his brother in vain:* [93] the addition *in vain* shows that the use of anger is often opportune, namely, whenever this passion is roused for the chastisement of sin. The Word of Scripture has borne witness to this kind of wrath before in the case of Phineas [94] when he propitiated God who had threatened the people, by killing the transgressors of the Law.

He then passes on to the healing of the sins committed for the sake of pleasure, and, by His commandment, frees the heart from the vile desire of adultery. Thus you will find in what follows how the Lord corrects them all one by one, opposing by His Law each one of the forms of evil. He prevents the beginning of unjust violence by not even permitting self-defence. He banishes the passion of avarice by ordering a man who has been robbed and stripped to give up also what is left to him. He heals cowardice by commanding to scorn death. And, in general, you will find that by means of each of these commandments the Word digs up the evil roots from the depths of our hearts as if by a plough, and so through them we are purged from bringing forth thorns.

Therefore He does good to our nature in either way, by promising good things as well as by giving us the teaching that answers this purpose. But if the pursuit of goodness seem irksome to you, compare it with the opposite way of life, and you will find how much more painful it is to be wicked, that is, if you look not to the present but to what comes hereafter. For when one hears the word "hell," one will no longer avoid sinful pleasures sadly and with difficulty; the fear that is present in the thought alone will suffice to chase away the passions. It might be useful to consider what is implicitly contained in the teaching, so that this may kindle in us a stronger desire. For if the clean of heart are blessed, those with sordid minds are altogether miserable, because they look at the face of the adversary. Further, if the Divine character itself is impressed on the virtuous life, it is clear that the evil life resembles the form and face of the enemy. Now, according to different concepts, God is called by those representing the good, for example, light, life, incorruption, and similar things. By contrast, everything opposed to these is dedicated to the instigator of evil, for example, darkness, death, corruption, and whatever else is like to these. Hence, as we have learned what is an evil life and what is a good one—for we have it in the power of our free will to choose either of these—let us flee from the form of the devil, let us lay aside the evil mask and put on again the Divine Image. Let us become clean of heart, so that we may become blessed when the Divine Image is formed in us through purity of life, in Christ Jesus Our Lord, to whom be glory for ever and ever. Amen.

Blessed are the peacemakers, for they shall be called sons of God.

Moses the Lawgiver fashioned the sacred Tabernacle [95] for the Israelites according to the pattern which God had shown him on the mountain. Whatever was contained within the sanctuary was pure and sacred; but its innermost part was *adyton* [96] and inaccessible and was called the Holy of Holies. I think this more emphatic appellation shows that the sacredness of this part was not the same as that of the others; but inasmuch as something that has been duly consecrated differs from what is common and profane, the *adyton* is of purer holiness than the sacred places around it. This I believe also to be the case with the Beatitudes that have been shown us on this mountain. All that the Divine Word has so far laid down is indeed perfectly holy. But what we are now invited to contemplate is truly *adyton*, and the Holy of Holies. For if the blessedness of seeing God cannot be surpassed, to become the son of God transcends bliss altogether. For what do the words mean? What terms would suffice to exhaust the gift of so great a promise? Whatever the mind may conceive, what is signified is completely above it. If you call that which the Beatitude promises good, or glorious, or sublime, yet what is made known is something more than these words mean: it is fulfilment that outstrips prayer, gift surpassing hope, grace transcending nature. What is man compared with the Divine Nature? Which Saint's words shall I quote to prove that human nature is held in low esteem? According to Abraham it is dust and ashes,[97] according to Isaias, grass.[98] David does not actually call it grass, but "as" grass.[99] For the one says, *All flesh is grass*, the other, *Man is as grass*. Ecclesiastes says it is *vanity*,[100] St. Paul, *misery*.[101] For the whole human race bemoans its fate in the words the Apostle uses for his own person.

This is man. But what is God? How shall I name that which can neither be seen nor heard, nor comprehended by the heart? By which words shall I make known His Nature? Where among the things we know can I find a likeness of this greatest good? What new words can I coin so as to describe the wholly inexpressible? I have heard the Divinely inspired Scriptures disclose marvellous things about the transcendent Nature—yet what are they compared with that Nature Itself? For even if I were capable of grasping all that the Scripture says, yet that which is signified is more. For when we breathe in the air according to the space that is in each of us, one will receive more air, the other, less; yet he who takes in much has not absorbed the whole element into himself; but he, too, has only taken from the whole as much as he could, while the whole is still there.

So it is also with the words said about God in Holy Scripture, which are expounded to us by men inspired by the Holy Spirit. If measured by our understanding, they are indeed exalted above all greatness; yet they do not reach the majesty of the truth. *Who has measured heaven with a span, and water in his hand, and all the earth in his palm?* [102] Do you see by what majestic words he describes the transcendent power? Yet what are they compared with the reality? For despite these magnificent terms the words of the prophet show but part of the Divine Energy. He does not name the Power Itself from which springs this Energy, to say nothing of the Nature from which comes the Power; nor would he name it. Rather does he by these words rebuke those who attempt some representation of the Divinity; for, speaking in the Person of God, he says, *To whom have you likened me? saith the Lord.*[103] Ecclesiastes puts the same injunction in his own words: *Utter not a word hastily before God; for God is in heaven above, and thou on the earth below.*[104] By the distance of these elements from each other he intends to show, I suppose, how far the Divine Nature surpasses earthly thoughts. Man is esteemed as nothing, as ashes and grass and vanity among the things that exist, yet he becomes akin to this great Majesty that can neither be seen nor heard nor thought; he is received as a son by the God of the universe.

How can one give thanks worthily for such a gift? With what words, what thoughts that move our mind can we praise this abundance of grace? Man transcends his own nature, he who was subject to corruption in his mortality, becomes immune from it in his immortality, eternal from being fixed in time—in a word, a god from a man. For if he is made worthy of becoming a son of God, he will possess in himself the dignity of the Father and be made heir of all the Father's goods. How munificent is this rich Lord! How generously He opens His Hands wide to give us His ineffable treasures! Through His love of man He brings our nature, dishonoured by sin, to an honour that almost equals His own. For if He brings man into relationship with what He Himself is by nature, what else does He promise but a certain equality of honour due to such kinship?

So great, then, is the prize of the contest. But what is this contest? If you are a peacemaker, He says, you will be crowned with the grace of adoption as a son. It seems to me that the work, for which so great a reward is promised, is itself also a gift. For which of the things men desire is sweeter than a peaceful life? Whatever you may mention of the pleasant things of life, it needs peace in order to be pleasant.

Supposing one had all the things that are held dear in this life; riches, good health, wife and children, a house, one's parents, servants, and friends. Add to this produce from land and sea, pleasant gardens and venison, imagine even baths and boxing rings, gymnasiums and places where youth can amuse itself, and whatever other things there may be invented for pleasure. Add yet further attractive shows and musical recitals and anything else that makes life pleasant for those who live in luxury. If all this is there, yet the blessing of peace be absent, what good are these fine things if war cuts short their enjoyment? Therefore peace itself is sweet to enjoy, and sweetens all that is held dear in life. And even if we suffer any human misfortune, as long as there is peace the evil is borne more easily, because it is mixed with some good; but if life is haunted by war, we become in a way insensible even to our own occasions of grief. For the common calamity is greater than the individual causes of pain.

Doctors tell us something similar in the case of physical ailments. If two diseases coincide in the same body, only the stronger one makes itself felt, whereas the pain caused by the lesser illness remains latent, since it is overlaid by the attack of the more virulent one. Thus also the more poignant evils of war make individuals insensible to their own misfortunes. But if the soul becomes somehow insensible even to its own woes, because the common evils of war have struck panic into it, how can it still savour what is pleasant? For now there are everywhere arms and horses, iron and sounds of trumpets. Men are in battle array, bristling with spears; shields are clanging together and crests nod from their helmets inspiring fear. There are single encounters, close fights, hand-to-hand wrestlings, battles where men are slaughtered, flee and are pursued. There are noisy laments, the earth is moist with blood, the dead are trodden under foot and the wounded abandoned —all those grim atrocities connected with war.

Can one who is involved in such things ever give his mind to any joyful memory? And even if sometimes the thought of something lovely steals into his soul, will he not at once remember that his dearest ones are in danger, and will not this thought that creeps into his mind add to his unhappiness? Therefore, when He rewards you if you keep away from the evils of war, He bestows a double gift on you. For one gift is the reward of the contest, the other is the contest itself. So even if no further hope was promised a man, those who have sense would prize peace for its own sake above all else.

By this, therefore, one can see how greatly He loves man, that He bestows the precious reward not on pains and sweat, but, so to speak, on the enjoyment of happiness. Peace is indeed the greatest of the joy-giving things; and this He wishes each of us to have in such measure as to keep it not only for himself, but to be able to dispense from the overflow of his abundance also to others. For

He says, *Blessed are the peacemakers*. Now a peacemaker is a man who gives peace to another; but one cannot give another what one does not possess oneself. Hence the Lord wants you first to be yourself filled with the blessings of peace, and then to communicate it to those who have need of it.

And our sermon need not be too much concerned with the profound spiritual sense [105] of the passage; the obvious meaning is all we need to acquire this marvellous thing. *Blessed are the peacemakers*—these words give us the cure of many diseases as it were in a nutshell, for all the individual things are contained in its comprehensive universality.

Let us first consider what peace is. Surely it is nothing else but a loving disposition towards one's neighbour. Now what is held to be the opposite of love? [106] It is hate and wrath, anger and envy, harbouring resentment as well as hypocrisy and the calamity of war. Do you see for how many different diseases this single word is an antidote? For peace is equally opposed to every one of the things mentioned, and wipes out these evils by its own presence. Just as illness vanishes when health supervenes, and as no darkness is left when light begins to shine, so also when peace appears, all the passions connected with its opposite are eliminated.

I do not think it is necessary here to elaborate in detail how great a good this is. You can think over for yourself what kind of life those lead who treat each other with jealousy and hatred. Their conversations are unpleasant; they abominate all mutual intercourse; their mouths make no sound, their eyes are turned away from each other, and their hearing is blocked to the voice of him who hates and is himself hated. Whatever is dear to the one is not so to the other, and conversely, whatever is hated and detested by the one is acceptable to his enemy. Therefore He wants the grace of peace fully to abound in you like the pleasant scent of sweet spices that fills the air around it with its own fragrance, so that your life may heal the sickness of others.

How great a good this is you will know more clearly if you consider the ravages produced in the soul by all the passions connected with hate. Who could expose adequately the vicious effects of wrath? Which sermon could describe how shameful is this disease? You see the passions of the possessed appear in those dominated by wrath. Consider side by side the symptoms of the demon and the symptoms of wrath, and what difference there is between the two. The eye of the demoniac is bloodshot and distracted, his tongue is unsteady and his speech harsh, his voice sounds sharp like barking. These symptoms are common both to wrath and to the demon. His head, too, is tossed about wildly, his hands make senseless movements, his whole body shakes and his feet are wobbling— this whole description is the same for both diseases. They differ from each other only in this, that the one evil is voluntary, whereas the other happens to its victims against their will. But how much more miserable is it to be in this predicament through one's own fault than to suffer it involuntarily! Moreover, if one sees that the disease is caused by the demon, it will certainly arouse pity; but if the derangement is produced by wrath, the man who sees it at once also imitates it, as if he lost something if he did not outdo the first sufferer in his own disease. If the demon racks the body of an afflicted man, the evil goes no further than vainly throwing about the hands of the maniac in the air; whereas the demon of wrath causes no useless bodily movements. For when the passion lays hold of a man and the heartblood boils over, when wrath, as they say, makes the black gall diffuse itself throughout the body, then all the senses that are placed in the head are affected with cramp by the compression of the internal vapours. The eyes protrude from under their confining lids, staring bloodshot like dragons at the offending object; the inside is compressed, panting for breath, the veins in the throat swell and the tongue thickens. Since the windpipe is straitened, the voice automatically becomes rasping; the diffusion of the cold bile causes the lips to go all stiff and black, and they find it difficult to open and close in the natural way, so that they cannot even control the spittle that overflows in the mouth, but emit it together with the words, and while gasping out the sound dribble froth as well. Then one will also see the hands and feet being tossed about by the disease; but the limbs are no longer thrown about aimlessly, as happens with the demoniacs, but in order to inflict harm on those wrestling with each other in the grip of this illness. For when they hit each other, their attacks are immediately directed against the vital organs. And if in the close fight the mouth perchance approaches the other's body, even the teeth do not remain idle but, after the manner of wild beasts, are dug into anyone who comes near.

But who could recount in detail all the evil that comes from wrath? Therefore a person who prevents such disgrace may truly be called blessed and should be honoured for such beneficial action. For if someone who has relieved a man from some physical ailment is honoured for his good deed, how much more should every sensible person consider a benefactor him who has freed the soul from this disease? Inasmuch as the soul is superior to the body, the man who cures souls is more honourable than those who heal bodies.

Let no one imagine that I consider the viciousness of wrath the gravest of the evils produced by hatred. Envy and hypocrisy seem to me much worse diseases than the one just mentioned, since a hidden evil is more dangerous than one that is obvious. In the case of dogs, too, we beware more of those whose fury is not announced in advance by their barking, so that their attack does not seem imminent, but who, under a pleasantly gentle appearance, wait for us to be unsuspecting and off our guard. Such is the disease of envy and hypocrisy; it is cherished secretly in the depth of the heart, like a hidden fire, while externally everything is made to look deceptively like friendship. It is like a fire that is hidden under chaff. For a time it smoulders inside and burns only what lies near; the flame does not flare up visibly, only a biting smoke penetrates, because it is so vigorously compressed from within. But if it meets with some gust of wind, it is rekindled into a bright open flame. Thus envy, too, consumes the heart from within like fire that is kept down by a pile of chaff. A man may hide his disease for shame, yet he cannot conceal it forever; but like a certain acrid smoke the bitterness that springs from envy is given away by telltale looks and mien. If the envied person meets with some misfortune, then he reveals his disease, because he makes that man's sorrow his own joy and pleasure.

Yet even while it still seems to be hidden, the secret disease betrays itself by visible indications in the face. For the symptoms of a person pining away with envy are the same as the signs of death in someone who has been given up; such as dry, hollow eyes within shrivelled lids, contracted eyebrows and bones showing in some places through the flesh. And what is the cause of this disease? That a brother or a friend or a neighbour lives happily. What unheard-of offences! To make it a ground of complaint that someone is not unhappy, merely because one is grieved by this man's joy. Not that oneself had suffered any evil from that man which he could imagine to be wrong, but simply because that other man suffers no harm and lives as he likes. What have you suffered, you miserable creature—I would like to say to him—why are you in fits, glowering with an evil eye at the good fortune of your neighbour? What have you to complain of? That he is good-looking, gifted with eloquence, and of better family? That he has taken over an office which has brought him conspicuous dignity? That a windfall of wealth has come to him, or that he is honoured because of his prudent speech? Do you envy him because he is admired by the crowds as a benefactor, or because he is proud of his children, happy with his wife, and distinguishes himself by entertaining in his house? Why do these things pierce your heart like the barbs of arrows? You rub your palms in anger, you clench your fists, you are troubled in mind. You groan painfully from the depths, you find no pleasure in the enjoyment of the things at your disposal, your meals are tasteless, your hearth is gloomy, and your ears are ready to hear the happy man slandered. But if anything good be said about him, to such words you shut your ears.

Now if you are in such a state of mind, why do you put the cloak of hypocrisy round your disease? Why do you counterfeit the mask of friendship and fake well-wishing? Why do you welcome people with pleasant words, wishing them happiness and good health, while in your mind you silently imprecate the opposite? Such a man was Cain who raved when Abel was praised. The envy within commanded the murder, but hypocrisy became its executioner; for under the guise of a friendly and pleasant manner he led him out into the field far from the help of his parents, and then he revealed his envy by murder. Therefore a man who eliminates such a disease from man's life and unites the members of the same race by peace and goodwill, truly performs a work of Divine power; for he banishes the evils of human nature and introduces instead a share in what is good. For this reason He calls the peacemaker a son of God, because he imitates the true God, who endows human life with these blessings.

Therefore, *Blessed are the peacemakers, for they shall be called sons of God.* Who are these? Those who imitate the Divine love of men, who show forth in their own life the characteristic of the Divine energy. The Lord and Giver of good things completely annihilates anything that is without affinity and foreign to goodness. This work He ordains also for you, namely to cast out hatred and abolish war, to exterminate envy and banish strife, to take away hypocrisy and extinguish from within resentment of injuries smouldering in the heart. Instead, you ought to introduce whatever is contrary to the things that have been removed. For as light follows the departure of darkness, thus also these evil things are replaced by the fruits of the Spirit,[107] by charity, joy, peace, benignity, magnanimity, all the good things enumerated by the Apostle. How then should the Dispenser of the Divine gifts not be blessed, since he imitates the gifts of God and models his own good deeds on the Divine munificence?

But perhaps the Beatitude does not only regard the good of others. I think that man is called a peacemaker *par excellence* who pacifies perfectly the discord between flesh and spirit in himself and the war that is inherent in nature, so that the law of the body no longer wars against the law of the mind, but is subjected to the higher rule and becomes a servant of the Divine ordinance. We should, however, beware of thinking that, because the Word counsels this, the life of the virtuous is conceived as a duality;[108] on the contrary, when the partition wall of evil that blocks us up has been taken away, the two will become one and coalesce, because both are united to the good. Since, therefore, the Divine is believed not to be composite but simple and without counterfeit, by such peacemaking human nature, too, goes beyond its twofold composition; it returns completely to the good and becomes simple and free from deceit. Thus it is made truly one, so that what appears is the same as what is hidden, and what is hidden the same as what appears. Then the Beatitude has come true, for such men are verily called sons of God, since they are called blessed according to the promise of Our Lord Jesus Christ, to whom be glory for ever and ever. Amen.

SERMON 8

Blessed are they that suffer persecution for justice' sake, for theirs is the Kingdom of Heaven.

Following the order of the sublime teaching of doctrine, the present interpretation of the words is led on to the eighth step. But I think it opportune that we should first consider in our sermon what is the mystery of the number eight, which the prophet mentions in two Psalms,[109] and what is the meaning of the purification and the legislation concerning circumcision, which, according to the Law, were both to be observed on the eighth day. Perhaps this number has some affinity with the eighth Beatitude, which, being as it were the summit of all the Beatitudes, is placed at the top of the glorious ascent. For in the Psalms the prophet signifies the Day of the Resurrection through the mystery of the number eight; the purification indicates man's return from defilement to his natural purity; the circumcision means the casting off of the dead skins [110] which we put on when we had been stripped of the supernatural life after the transgression; and here the eighth Beatitude contains the re-instatement in heaven of those who had fallen into servitude, and who are now from their slavery recalled to the Kingdom.

Blessed, He says, *are those who suffer persecution* for my sake, *for theirs is the Kingdom of Heaven.* Here is the goal of the battles fought for God, here the reward of the labours, the prize of our sweat, which is to be held worthy of the Kingdom of Heaven. No longer do we go astray, pinning our hope on what is unstable and subject to change. For earth is the place of variation and flux; but in the things that appear moving in heaven we observe nothing like that, because they do not behave in such a way; but all heavenly things move in their own courses in series of orderly sequence. Do you then see how excellent is the gift? For its magnificence is not made up of variable things, so that no fear of change should trouble our fair hopes; but by saying *Kingdom of Heaven* He shows the absolute immutability of the gift that is held out to our expectation.

But some difficulty has come into my mind about what has been said. It is this. First: to both, those who are poor in spirit and those who are persecuted for His sake, He promises as a reward to bring them to the same goal. Now if their prize is to be the same, surely their struggles, too, must be equal. Secondly: why, in the passage where He calls men to the Kingdom of Heaven and separates the ones on the right from those on the left,[111] does He give other reasons for such an honour? For there He demands compassion, mutual assistance, and love; but nowhere does He mention spiritual poverty or persecution for His sake; yet, considered superficially, these things seem greatly to differ from each other. For what has poverty to do with persecution? Or again, what connection have these with the charitable deeds of compassion? Someone has fed the needy or clothed the naked, he has received the stranger under his roof or has brought the sick and the prisoners what help he could—but what has this to do with being oneself poor and persecuted, according to the passage we are considering? This man helps others in their misfortunes, on the other hand both the poor and the persecuted need themselves help—yet the goal is in every respect the same. For He brings to Heaven the poor in spirit and the one who is persecuted for His sake, as well as those who show compassion for their neighbour. How then do we explain this? It all hangs together, for they all converge on precisely the same goal. Poverty is easily transferred, and the love of the poor is not far removed from poverty itself. But I think it best first to examine the present passage, and then to look closer into the meaning and agreement of the words we have been considering.

Blessed are they who suffer persecution for justice' sake. Why and by whom are they persecuted? The answer that comes first into our mind clearly presents to us the arena of the martyrs and the race-course of the faith. For the pursuit shows up not only the runner's intense concern for speed, but it also makes clear the victory that lies in running, since the runner cannot gain it otherwise but by leaving behind the person that runs with him. Hence both the man who runs for the prize of the supernal vocation, and the one who is persecuted by the enemy on account of this prize, have someone behind them, the one the person contending with him, the other the persecutor. Now these are the men who accomplish the course of martyrdom and who are pursued, but not caught, in the contests of piety. It seems that in the last words He holds out to them the highest Beatitude like a crown. For it is truly blessed to suffer persecution for the sake of the Lord. And why? Because being chased by evil becomes the cause of attaining to the good, since separation from the wicked one is made the occasion for drawing near to the Good, that Good that is above every good, the Lord Himself, to whom runs the man who is persecuted. Therefore he is truly blessed, because he uses the enemy to help him attain the Good. Human life lies between the boundaries of good and evil; and as a man who has abandoned the transcendent Good of our hope has sunk into the pit, so he who becomes an utter stranger to the corruption of sin approaches incorruptible Justice.

Hence the immediate aspect of the persecution which tyrants unleash against the martyrs is indeed painful to the senses; but the outcome of it exceeds all beatitude. Perhaps we may better grasp the sense of the passage by giving examples. Everyone knows how hard it is to bear if people, instead of loving us, scheme against us. Yet there are many for whom that which had seemed harmful becomes the cause of happiness even in this life. This is shown by the story of Joseph. His brothers plotted against him and drove him away from their company. But through being sold he became the king of those who had planned evil against him, and he would perhaps not have attained to such great dignity, had not their envy paved the way for the kingdom by this very plot. Now if someone who knew the future had foretold Joseph: You will be blessed because a plot has been devised against you, this would not have seemed immediately credible to the hearer, who would see only the present distress; for he would not have thought it possible that the evil purpose could come to a good end. So also in the present instance, the fact that the persecution the tyrants inflict on the faithful brings much sensible pain, makes it difficult for the more carnally-minded to accept the hope of the Kingdom that is to be realized through these pains. But the Lord, who looks down upon the infirmity of our nature, tells the weak beforehand what is to be the goal of the struggle, so that they may more easily overcome the transitory feelings of pain.

Therefore the great Stephen rejoices when he is stoned from all sides. His body eagerly receives the showers of fast-falling stones like a pleasant dew, and he repays his murderers with blessings, praying that the sin may not be imputed to them. He, too, has heard the promise and has seen the hope that corresponds to the things that happen in the world of sense. For he first heard that those who suffer persecution for the sake of the Lord will be in the Kingdom of Heaven, and then he saw the object of his expectation at the moment of persecution. While he was running the race of confessing the faith, he was shown what he hoped for, the heavens opened and the Divine Glory looking down from the transcendent realm on the struggle of the runner, that is to say, the Lord Himself to whom the struggle of His martyr bears witness. Now the standing posture of the Judge of the struggle is an image revealing the help He gives to the fighter, by which we should learn that the same Person who ordains the contest also assists His own fighters against their opponents. Who, therefore, could be more blessed than the man who is persecuted for the sake of the Lord, and who is privileged to have as his helper the Judge Himself, who presides at the contest?

For it is not easy, in fact, perhaps quite impossible, to prefer the invisible Good to the visible pleasant things of this life, so as easily to choose things like being driven from one's home or separated from wife and children, brothers, parents and friends, and all the happiness of life, unless the Lord Himself helps him to attain to this Good, because he has been called according to His purpose. *For,* as the Apostle says, *whom He foreknows, him He also predestinates, and calls, and justifies, and glorifies.*[112] Now the soul is in some way attached to the pleasant things of life through the senses of the body. Through the eyes it delights in material beauty, through the ears it inclines to melodious sounds, and so it is also affected by smell, taste, and touch, as nature has disposed to be proper to each. Hence, as it is attached to the pleasant things of life through the sensible faculty as if by a nail, it is hard to turn away from them. It has grown up together with these attachments much in the same way as the shellfish and snails are bound to their covering of clay; and so it is slow to make such movements, since it drags along the whole burden of a lifetime. As such is its condition, the soul is easily captured by its persecutors with the threat of confiscation of property or loss of some other things that are coveted in this life; and so it gives in easily, and yields to the power of its persecutor.

But when the living Word which, as the Apostle says, *is effectual and more piercing than any two-edged sword,*[113] penetrates into a man who has truly received the faith, it cuts through the things that have badly grown together, and disrupts the fetters of habit. Then he will throw off the worldly pleasures bound to his soul, like a runner casts a burden from his shoulders, and will run light and nimble through the fighting ring, since he is guided in his course by the President of the contest Himself. For he looks not to the things he has left behind, but to those that come hereafter, and so he does not turn back his eyes to the pleasures that are past, but he goes forward to the Good that lies before him. He is not pained by the loss of earthly things, but gladdened by the gain of heavenly ones. Therefore he will readily accept every form of torture as a means that will help him to attain to the joy before him: the fire, as a purification from matter; the sword, as disrupting the union of the mind with what is material and carnal. Every device for inflicting pain he will receive eagerly as an antidote against the dangerous poison of pleasure. The bilious and those suffering from superfluous humours readily drink the bitter medicine by which the cause of the disease might be removed. In the same way a man who, persecuted by the enemy, turns to God, accepts the onrush of sufferings as a means of destroying the power of pleasure.

For a man who suffers cannot enjoy pleasure. Hence, as sin entered through pleasure, it is exterminated by the opposite. So if men persecute others for confessing the Lord and invent the most intolerable tortures, they bring, through these sufferings, a remedy to souls, for by applying pain they heal the disease caused by pleasure. Thus Paul receives the cross, James the sword; Stephen the stones, the blessed Peter is crucified head downwards.[114] All the later fighters for the faith suffer many forms of torture, being thrown to the beasts and into pits, being burned with fire or frozen with cold, having their sides flayed and their heads transfixed by nails; or their eyes are put out, their fingers cut off, their bodies are rent in two by their legs being pulled apart, or they suffer starvation. All these and other things like them the Saints have embraced with joy as a purification from sin. And so pleasure has left no trace impressed on the heart, for the piercing sensation of pain effaced all the imprints it had stamped on the soul. Therefore, *Blessed are those who suffer persecution* for my sake.

Now let us also proffer another consideration. It is the same as if someone, speaking in the person of health, were to say: Blessed are those that are separated from disease for my sake. They are without pains, and so it happens that those who were once sick are now resting in me. Therefore let us give heed to the Voice, since Life itself is announcing this Beatitude to us. Blessed are those who are persecuted by death for my sake. It is as if light said: Blessed are those who are persecuted by darkness for my sake. The same may be said of justice and sanctity, of incorruption and goodness, in fact, of any concept of those things that thought associates with the Good. We can imagine the Lord speaking to you somewhat like this: Blessed is the man who is driven away from all that is hostile, from corruption, darkness, and sin, from injustice and covetousness, in short, from anything that is not virtuous, whether in words, deeds, or thoughts. For to be separated from evil means being confirmed in goodness. *Whosoever committeth sin,* says the Lord, *is the servant of sin.*[115] Hence, if a man leaves what he used to serve, he attains to the dignity of a freeman. For the highest form of freedom is to be master of oneself. Now the dignity of kingship has no dictator above it. If, therefore, a man who is a stranger to sin is free, and if, on the other hand, the property of kingship is to be self-governing and without a master; it follows that a man who is persecuted by evils is blessed, because persecution from that quarter procures for him the royal dignity.

Let us therefore not be depressed, my brethren, if we are deprived of earthly things. For if a man is released from these, he lives in the palaces of Heaven. The rational nature has been allotted two elements of the created universe—earth and Heaven—for its life. The place of those who have received life in the flesh is the earth, whereas Heaven is the abode of the immaterial beings. Now our life must necessarily be lived somewhere. If we are not chased away from the earth, we surely remain on earth. But when we depart from here, we shall be translated to Heaven. Do you see where this Beatitude brings you, since it helps you to achieve so great a good by means of apparent suffering? The Apostle also had perceived this when he says: *All chastisement for the present indeed seemeth not to bring with it joy, but sorrow; but afterwards it will yield to them that are exercised by it the peaceable fruit of justice.*[116]

Therefore affliction is the flower that will yield the hoped-for fruits. Hence let us pick the flower for the sake of the fruit. Let us be persecuted so that we may run, but if we run, let us not run in vain. Let us race towards the prize of our supernal vocation; *so let us run that we may obtain.*[117] What is it that we shall obtain? What is the prize, what the crown? It seems to me that what we hope is nothing else but the Lord Himself. For He Himself is the Judge of those who fight, and the crown of those who win. He it is who distributes the inheritance, He Himself is the goodly inheritance. He is the portion and the giver of the portion, He makes rich and is Himself the riches. He shows you the treasure and is Himself your treasure. He draws you to desire the beautiful pearl; He offers it to you as it were for sale, if you will trade fairly. In order to gain it, therefore, as if in the market, let us compare the things we have not with those we have. Let us not be sorrowful, then, if we are persecuted, but rather let us rejoice, because by being chased away from earthly honours, we are driven towards the heavenly Good. For this He has promised, that those who have been persecuted for His sake shall be blessed, for theirs is the Kingdom of Heaven, by the grace of Our Lord Jesus Christ, to whom be glory and power for ever and ever. Amen.

NOTES

INTRODUCTION

[1] *Ep.* 13 (MG 46.1049A ff.).

[2] Ch. 3 (MG 46.326A, B).

[3] *Ep.* 197 (MG 37.324A).

[4] Basil, *Ep.* 100.

[5] Mai, A., *Scripta vet. nova coll.* 7 (Rome 1833) pars 1, p. 6 f.

[6] Krabinger, J. G., *S. Gregorii episc. Nyss. De precatione orationes* 5 (Landeshut 1840) 62–64.

[7] Oehler, F., *Bibliothek der Kirchenväter* 1.3 (Leipzig 1859) 262–64. The latest edition is found in F. Diekamp, *Doctrina Patrum de incarnatione Verbi* (Münster i.W. 1907) 4–7.

[8] K. Holl, *Amphilochius von Ikonium in seinem Verhältnis zu den grossen Kappadoziern* (Tübingen–Leipzig 1904) 215.

[9] F. Diekamp, *Theol. Rev.* 3 (1904) 332.

[10] Cf. R. Leys, *L'image de Dieu chez saint Grégoire de Nysse. Esquisse d'une doctrine* (Museum Lessianum, sect. théol. 49, Brussels-Paris 1951).

[11] Cf. G. Horn, "Le miroir, la nuée, deux manières de voir Dieu d'après S. Grégoire de Nysse," *Revue d'Asc. et de Myst.* 8 (1927) 113–31.

[12] Cf. *De beat.* 6.

[13] Cf. Gregory of Nyssa, *In Cant.* hom. 15.

[14] See F. Diekamp, *Die Gotteslehre des hl. Gregor von Nyssa* 1 (Münster i.W. 1896) 83–86; H. F. Cherniss, *The Platonism of Gregory of Nyssa* (Univ. of California Publications in Class. Philol. 11, Berkeley 1934); J. Daniélou, *Platonisme et théologie mystique. Essai sur la doctrine spirituelle de saint Grégoire de Nysse* (Paris 1944).

TEXT

THE LORD'S PRAYER

[1] See Rom. 12.2.

[2] See Col. 3.5: *Mortificate . . . avaritiam, quae est simulacrorum servitus* (cf. Eph. 5.5). For a detailed exposition of this equation, covetousness = idolatry, see John Chrysostom, *In Rom. hom.* 6.6. In the following Gregory develops rather the statement made by St. Paul elsewhere (1 Tim. 6.10) that avarice is the root of all evil.

[3] πάθος — a word of many different shades of meaning, without a real equivalent in English. It played an important part in Stoic philosophy, whence the Greek Fathers took it over, attaching to it very frequently the sense of something sinful. Thus Clement of Alexandria (*Prot.* 11.115.2) defines πάθη as ψυχῆς νόσοι, "diseases of the soul," and Methodius (*Symp.* 8.16) speaks of πάθη as τῶν ἁμαρτημάτων αἴτια, "responsible for sin." Hence they are incompatible with the perfect Christian life: cf. Clement, *Strom.* 6.9.76.4; Elias Ecdicus, Cap. al. 178. They are healed by Christ: Justin Martyr, *2 Apol.* 13.4. The later Fathers lay particular stress on their conquest by ascetical practices (so e. g. Nilus, *Exerc.* 24; Maximus Confessor, *Carit.* 2.47), through which the spiritual "athlete" will arrive at freedom from πάθη — ἀπάθεια, for which see below, nn. 19 and 68. On πάθη in the writings of Clement, cf. W. Völker, *Der wahre Gnostiker nach Clemens Alexandrinus* (Berlin-Leipzig) 181–219.

[4] Luke 18.1.

[5] The ancient pagan practice of bride and bridegroom wearing chaplets or crowns at their wedding appears to have been frowned upon during the first two centuries of Christianity (cf. esp. Tertullian, *De corona* 13). In Gregory's time, however, the wedding crown (στέφανος νυμφικός) no longer offended Christian sensibilities. When this crown was placed on the Christian entering marriage, its immemorial symbolism of victory was still preserved: Christians must enter marriage with their previous life

clean, with a record of victory won over concupiscence and temptation (cf. John Chrystostom, *In 1 Tim.* hom. 9.2). See K. Baus, *Der Kranz in Antike und Christentum* (Theophania 2, Bonn 1940) 93–112 (109 f.: retention today of the bridal "crowning" in the Byzantine liturgy).

[6] For the events referred to see Jonas 2; 4 Kings 20.2 ff.; Dan. 3.24 ff.; Exod. 17.11 ff.; 4 Kings 19.14–35.

[7] Cf. Acts 17.28.

[8] εἰκών, the image of God in which man was made, according to Gen. 1.26. It plays a very important part in the mystical theology of the Greek Fathers, who speculated especially on the exact characteristic by which man reflects the Divine. The Alexandrian school, that is to say, Clement and Origen and their disciples, place it in the soul as the rational part of man: εἰκὼν... τοῦ Θεοῦ ὁ λόγος αὐτοῦ... εἰκὼν δὲ τοῦ λόγου ὁ ἄνθρωπος ὁ ἀληθινός, ὁ νοῦς ὁ ἐν ἀνθρώπῳ—so Clement, *Prot.* 10.98.3; Origen, *C. Cels.* 6.63. Irenaeus, *Adv. haer.* 4.4.3, saw in it man's free will; Gregory held it to consist especially in freedom from necessity; he placed the creation κατ' εἰκόνα before the distinction of the sexes which, according to him, was not in the original Divine plan for mankind but came in later as a result of God's foreknowledge of the Fall. See for this especially the 16th chapter of his *De hominis opificio*. According to one opinion the Image was lost through the Fall, so e. g. Tatian, *Or.* 7.3; Pseudo-Macarius, *Hom. spir.* 12.1; Gregory of Nyssa, *De virg.* 12. According to another, which has become the Catholic doctrine of the West, it was never lost; so Epiphanius, *Haer.* 70.2. The Image, whether lost or only defaced, is restored by the practice of virtue; so Clement, *Strom.* 2.19.102.2; Origen, *In Lev.* hom. 4.3. It becomes the seat of the contemplative life: Clement, *Strom.* 7.3.16.6; Gregory of Nyssa, *De beat.* 6 (cf. below, 146 ff.). See Völker, *op. cit.* 109–115; A. Lieske, *Die Theologie der Logosmystik bei Origenes* (Münsterische Beiträge zur Theologie 22, Münster i. W. 1938) 59 f., 100–103 ff., *passim*; R. Leys, *L'image de Dieu chez s. Grégoire de Nysse* (Brussels-Paris 1951).

[9] Rom. 3.11.

[10] Matt. 6.7: βατταλογέω, "babble," is an extremely rare word of uncertain derivation; G. Delling, in Kittel's *Theologisches Wörterbuch* 1 (1933) 597 f., thinks it most probable that it was formed on analogy of βατταρίζω, "stammer."

[11] ἐμπαθής, "impassioned," generally used in pejorative sense of souls subject to πάθος; see n. 3 above.

[12] Cf. Ps. 91.18, 67.3 etc.

[13] Jer. 10.25.

[14] Osee 9.14.

[15] Ps. 103.35.

[16] Cf. Gen. 1.27.

[17] Eph. 6.12.

[18] Ps. 34.4.

[19] ἀπαθής: see n. 68 on ἀπάθεια; also n. 3.

[20] Wisd. 1.13.

[21] Such false fronts were worn by Greek women from classical times.

[22] μυσταγωγία, initiation into (Divine) mysteries, a term in general use in the pagan mystery religions, whence it was taken over by the Fathers for the Christian "initiation" rite of baptism (so e. g. Basil, *De Spir. Sanct.* 75; Gregory of Nyssa, *De bapt. Christi:* MG46.584C; John Chrysostom, *In Ioann.* hom. 28.1) and also for any introduction to the knowledge of Divine things (e. g. Athanasius, *Exp. Ps.* 111.5; Cyril of Jerusalem, *Catech.* 19.11).   Hence Gregory likes to use it also in connection with the introduction of Moses, a type of Christ, to the contemplation of Jahweh on Mount Sinai; cf. also his *De vita Moys.*, e. g. MG 44.317A, C. The former sense, initiation into the sacred mysteries of Christianity through the reception of baptism, is illustrated particularly well in the celebrated *Mystagogical Catecheses* of Cyril of Jerusalem. In these lectures, given during the octave of Easter, the newly baptized were instructed on the mysteries—the sacraments—they had just received: baptism, confirmation, Eucharist (including the liturgy of the Mass). So too the *De mysteriis* of St. Ambrose serves the *mystagogical* instruction of Christian neophytes. For the texts of both Cyril and Ambrose, with introductions and notes, cf. J. Quasten, *Monumenta eucharistica et liturgica vetustissima* (Bonn 1935) 69–111, 113–177; for Cyril, F. L. Cross, *St. Cyril of Jerusalem's Lectures on the Christian Sacraments. The Procatechesis and the Five Mystagogical Catecheses* (London 1951).

[23] Sinai. See Exod. 19.

[24] For an allegorical treatment of this scene, see Gregory's *De vita Moys.*, esp. coll. 376 ff. Cf. above n. 22.

[25] εὔχομαι—εὐχή; προσεύχομαι—προσευχή. The root meaning of the former pair is *vow* (verb and substantive); of the latter, *pray* and *prayer*. The present passage refers to this distinction, which is brought out by several Fathers, e. g. Origen, *De or.* 4.1 f., and Maximus Confessor, *Quaest. ad Thalass.* 51 (MG 90. 469A). But commonly this distinction has become quite obliterated and both words are used in the same sense by the same author even in the same sentence.

[26] παρρησία, translated in the present work generally as *confidence* or *holy audacity*. In classical Greek it denoted the political freedom, especially the freedom of speech, claimed as their special privilege by the citizens of Athens. In the New Testament it is the quality of Apostles, preaching the Kingdom with παρρησία (Acts 28.31) and of Christians in general, whose faith in Christ gives them confidence (Heb. 3.6; 10.35), especially at the Second Coming (1 John 2.28) and in their prayer (1 John 5.14). In Patristic teaching παρρησία before God is closely related to freedom from sin and to sanctity in general; it was the characteristic of Adam and Eve before the Fall—so Methodius, *De resurr.* 2.25, Gregory of Nyssa, *De virg.* 12; *Or. catech.* 6; and of the great Old Testament Saints, e. g. Seth and Abel—so Methodius, *Symp.* 7.5—and especially of Moses, e. g. Origen, *De princ.* 3.1.22; John Chrysostom, *Adv. Iud.* hom. 8.6. In a very special way it is the quality of the martyrs who confess the faith with παρρησία before men and hence have παρρησία also before God, which makes their intercession particulary efficacious; so e. g. John Chrysostom, *Hom. in ss. mart. Beren. et Prosd.* 7; Asterius Amasenus, *Hom.* 10 (Mg 40.317C). Every Christian needs it in order to approach God in prayer, especially to say the Our Father. Cf. the present passage; also Chrysostom, *Exp. in Ps.* 4.1, Liturgy of St. James (Brightman p. 59.28); and the words before the Pater Noster in the Mass: *audemus* dicere.

[27] Ps. 65.13 f.

[28] *Ibid.* 75.12.

[29] Luke 11.2 (Matt. 6.9).

[30] Ps. 54.7.

[31] This description follows the Platonic conception of the various spheres by which the earth was held to be surrounded.

[32] 2 Cor. 6.14.

[33] Matt. 7.18.

[34] Ps. 4.3.
[35] Cf. John 8.44.
[36] Eph. 2.3.
[37] John 17.12.
[38] A reminiscence of Judith 16.12.
[39] 1 Thess. 5.5 (cf. Eph. 5.8).
[40] An adaptation from Rom. 1.4?
[41] 2 Cor. 6.14.
[42] Luke 15.21.
[43] The passage refers to the frequently occurring conception of the garments of skin χιτῶνες δερμάτινοι (Gen. 3.21), with which man was clothed after his disobedience. They are variously interpreted by the Fathers. Origen (cited by Theodoret, *Quaest. in Gen.* 39) sees in them the present human bodies, an interpretation widely rejected because it would imply that man had been created without a material body. Methodius (*De resurr.* 1.38), followed by Nilus (*Epist.* 2.241) and others, hold them to denote mortality. For Gregory they signify the whole of man's lower nature, comprising mortality, the passions, etc. Cf. especially *De an. et resurr.* (MG 46.148C) and J. Daniélou, *Platonisme et théologie mystique, Essai sur la doctrine spirituelle de S. Grégoire de Nysse* (Paris 1944), 60 ff.
[44] The concept as here introduced and discussed of striving to achieve resemblance, likeness to God, πρὸς τὸν Θεὸν ὁμοίωσις, is undoubtedly inspired by a celebrated passage in Plato's *Theaetetus* (176ab); cf. H. F. Cherniss, *The Platonism of Gregory of Nyssa*, Univ. Calif. Publ. Class. Philol. 11 (1930–1933) 47 f. (though already Krabinger, 135, mentions the passage in the *Theaet.*). See now H. Merki, ΟΜΟΙΩΣΙΣ ΘΕΩ, *Von der Platonischen Angleichung an Gott zur Gottähnlichkeit bei Gregor von Nyssa* (Paradosis 7, Fribourg 1952), where, 124–28, the present passage is discussed. Merki (127) offers quite convincing evidence that Gregory here is indebted rather to Plotinus, *Enn.* 1.2.1, than directly to Plato.
[45] Eccles. 5.1.
[46] Cf. Ps. 72.28.
[47] Matt. 5.48.
[48] John 1.12.
[49] ἡ ἐναντία φύσις, signifying the devil.
[50] Cf. Matt. 6.21.
[51] Rom. 2.11.

[52] Cf. Heb. 10.1.

[53] Cf. Exod. 28.4.39 (Lev. 8.7–12), the account of the vestments and anointing prescribed for Aaron as high priest.

[54] περισκελίς given as leg-band, garter, or anklet by Liddell and Scott, but more probably "breeches," as in Exod. 28.42.

[55] ἄδυτον, the Holy of Holies of the Temple, inaccessible to any save the high priest, which impenetrability made it a suitable symbol for the inner region of the soul, in which the mystical life is lived. Cf. especially Daniélou, *op. cit.* 195 ff.

[56] ἡγεμονικός, adj., more frequently as subst., ἡγεμονικόν, a term taken over from Stoic philosophy denoting the highest part of the soul. As in the present passage, it is often equated with mind or reason, e. g. by Tertullian, *De an.* 15, Clement of Alexandria, *Strom.* 2.11.51.6, Origen, *Comm. in Ioan.* fr. 18 (Preuschen); but from early times it has been accorded a special significance for the spiritual life, since it was intimately connected with the εἰκών (cf. above n. 8, and H. C. Graef, "L'Image de Dieu et la structure de l'âme d'après les Pères Grecs," in *La vie spir.*, suppl. 12 (1952) 331–39); so already Clement himself, *Strom.* 5.14.94.4; hence from Origen (cf. e. g. *C. Cels.* 4.66) onwards it is regarded as the seat of the spiritual life *par excellence*, on which prophetic and other visions are impressed; see Origen, *ibid.* 1.48; Ps.–Basil, *In Isa.* prooem. 3.

[57] μυστικός, a word of many connotations. Its root meaning (from μύω, *close the eyes*) is *secret, not easily accessible*, hence it is used for anything of a sacred character, e. g. the Tetragrammaton of the Hebrews (so Clement of Alexandria, *Strom.* 5.6.34.4), sacred grottoes (Eusebius, *Vita Const.* 3.43), etc., in particular for the most profound Christian doctrines, e. g. the Divinity of Christ (so Eusebius *Dem. Ev.* 3.7.141) and the Trinity (Cyril of Alexandria, *Fragm. dogmat.* 1 [MG 76.1424A]). It became a favourite term for the allegorical interpretation of Scripture (e. g. Clement, *Strom.* 5.6.37.1) and was popularized by Origen who used it constantly in this sense. In the later Fathers, μυστικός is used pre-eminently for the liturgical and sacramental life of the Church, as in the present passage; elsewhere in Gregory, e. g. *C. Eunom.* 11 (Jaeger 2.270.13) and *De bapt. Christi* (MG 46.581A); with special reference to baptism, Eusebius, *C. Marcell.* 1.1, and elsewhere; Gregory of Nyssa, *Or. catech.* 34; and throughout to the Eucharist, e. g. Gregory of Nazianzus, *Orat.* 40.31; Nilus, *Epist.* 2.233, etc. Our modern sense of "mys-

tical" is much more rare; it is to be found, especially as an epithet of θεωρία (contemplation), occasionally in Origen, e. g. *Comm. in Ioann.* 13.24.146, and Gregory of Nyssa, *In Cant.* hom. 1; also in Ps.-Macarius' *Spiritual Homilies,* in which (47.17) he speaks of a mystical communion of marriage. But its use in this sense was definitely established only by Ps.-Dionysius in connection with his negative theology, so e. g. *De div. nom.* 2.7; *De myst. theol.* 1.1. See also L. Bouyer, "Mystique, essai sur l'histoire d'un mot," *La vie spir.,* suppl. 9 (1949) 3.

⁵⁸ Cf. Eph. 6.17.

⁵⁹ Cf. Rom. 12.1.

⁶⁰ Ps. 68.15.

⁶¹ Cf. *ibid.* 55.10.

⁶² *Ibid.* 59.13 and 107.13.

⁶³ Cf. Isa. 40.12.

⁶⁴ Cf. Rom. 2:24 (Isa. 52.5, Ezech. 36.20).

⁶⁵ μυστήριον; the word was taken over from the pagan mystery religions, in which sense it is often used by the Fathers, e. g. Justin Martyr, *1 Apol.* 27.4; Tatian, *Orat. ad Graec.* 8.4, etc. The Christian religion was regarded by the pagans as just another such rite, and in this sense the word is here used. It was early adopted by the Christians for their own doctrines and rites. Ignatius, *Trall.* 2.3, speaks already of the deacons as dispensers of the mysteries of Christ, and Justin, *Dial.* 91.3, of the mystery of the Cross. At the same time as μυστικός (see above, n. 57), μυστήριον, too, came to be used of the sacraments, e. g. in reference to baptism, Eusebius, *Dem. Ev.* 9.6; Gregory of Nyssa, *Or. catech.* 33; to the Eucharist, Eusebius, *Dem. Ev.* 1.10; Chrysostom, *In 1 Cor.* hom. 23.2. The Latins first used *sacramentum,* with the same range of meaning as μυστήριον, which was also transliterated into *mysterium.* Cf. the article and literature by G. Bornkamm, "μυστήριον," Kittel's *Theol. Wörterb. z. N. T.* 4 (1942) 809–34; also J. de Ghellinck—E. de Backer—J. Poukens—G. Lebacqz, *Pour l'histoire du mot "sacramentum," I. Les Anténicéens* (Louvain—Paris 1924). Among the most recent literature on the subject I mention J. C. M. Fruytier, *Het woord* ΜΥΣΤΗΡΙΟΝ *in de Catechesen van Cyrillus van Jeruzalem* (Nijmegen 1950).

⁶⁶ Matt. 5.16.

⁶⁷ Ps. 67.3.

[68] ἀπάθεια, *absence of passions, detachment*, a term taken over from Stoic philosophy and applied both to God and to Christian Saints, whose highest state of perfection is to imitate the Divine ἀπάθεια. It is regarded as a characteristic of Christians, e. g. by Justin Martyr (*2 Apol.* 1.2). The Stoic ideal of the passionless philosopher was Christianized especially in Clement's conception of the true Gnostic, e. g. *Strom.* 4.22.137.3, and later by the Egyptian monks—cf. e. g. Palladius, *Hist. Laus.* prol. (Butler 2.12.3). It is generally considered indispensable for contemplation—so Origen, *Exp. in Prov.* 31.21; John Climacus devotes to it the 29th step of his *Ladder.* On the subject, cf. Völker, *op. cit.* 524–40 (Clement); G. Bardy, "Apatheia," *Dict. de spir. asc. et myst.* 1 (1937) 727–46; P. de Labriolle, "Apatheia," *Reallex. f. Ant. u. Christ.* 1 (1950) 482–87.

[69] A most rare variant of Luke 11.2; apparently also the reading in Marcion's text—cf. Tertullian, *Adv. Marc.* 4.26. It is found also in two minuscule MSS of the eleventh and twelfth centuries, which probably preserve the text followed by Gregory. When the variant is found in later Greek writers, e. g. Maximus Confessor, it is doubtless borrowed from Gregory. See Krabinger 141; B. F. Westcott—F. J. A. Hort, *The New Testament in the Original Greek; Appendix* (Cambridge 1870–76) 60; M. J. Lagrange, *Introduction à l'étude du Nouveau Testament; critique textuelle* (Paris 1935) 156.

[70] The whole passage refers to the Macedonian heresy, also called *Pneumatomachi*, who denied the divinity of the Holy Spirit. See G. Bardy, "Macédonius et les Macédoniens," *Dict. théol. cath.* 9.2 (1927) 1464–78.

[71] Θεομάχοι (cf. Acts 5.39), "fighters against God," reference to the Macedonians, as above.

[72] βασιλεία, the word for kingdom is the same as that for kingship in Greek. The argumentation from "Thy Kingdom come" to the sovereignty of the Holy Spirit can therefore not be adequately reproduced in English, as it depends on the double sense of the one Greek term.

[73] Heb. 1.3.

[74] That is, in the Arian controversy in which Gregory himself had taken part with his *Contra Eunomium.*

[75] The following doctrinal passage, from "Hence" to "into parts of different nature," is left out in most MSS and all editions save Krabinger. See Introd. 8–10.

⁷⁶ ὑπόστασις, lit. "that which underlies." It is a philosophical term, not defined with precision by Aristotle, who uses it in its ordinary sense of signifying objective reality as opposed to subjective delusions, whereas the Neo-Platonists, esp. Plotinus, employ it in their emanation theory for individual beings numerically different from each other (cf. *Enneads* 5). The term played a considerable part in the Trinitarian and Christological controversies of the 4th and 5th centuries. Owing to its second meaning, it was never unnatural to speak of the three hypostases of the Trinity, as the term safeguarded the unity of the Divine οὐσία (undifferentiated being) while admitting the difference of the relations between Father, Son, and Holy Spirit within the Triune God (cf. Basil's differentiation between ὑπόστασις and οὐσία in *Ep.* 235.6). In this sense the term is used already by Athanasius, *De virg.* 1; *Exp. fid.* 2 and *Tom. ad Antioch.* 5. This soon became the accepted terminology, cf. Basil, *Ep.* 38 *passim;* Gregory Nazianzenus, *Orat.* 39.11; Gregory of Nyssa, *C. Eunom.* 2 (vulg.) 13; Epiphanius, *Ancor.* 81.4; Chrysostom, *In Ioann.* hom. 4.1; Cyril of Alexandria, *C. Iulian.* 8; etc. In this sense the term is here used of the First Person of the Trinity.

In the Christological controversies it was used by Nestorius, who distinguished in Christ two ὑποστάσεις —cf. Cyril, *C. Orient.* 167A; a distinction which jeopardized the unity of His Person. The Monophysites, on the other hand, sacrificed the difference between the Divinity and the Humanity in Christ, so that orthodoxy had to be safeguarded by the Chalcedonian formula of the two φύσεις in the one ὑπόστασις. For the gradual development of the orthodox formula, see Cyril, *C. Theodoret.* 206BC, commented by Leontius of Byzantium, *C. Monophys.* (MG 86.1825A); Cyril, *Ep. oec.* anath. 3 and 4; Conc. Chalced., *Defin. fid.;* Leontius of Byzantium, *C. Nest.* 5.25; etc.

The two senses of the term are clearly defined by Leontius, *ibid.* 2.1, and John of Damascus, *Dial.* 42. Nevertheless their use gave rise to considerable confusion on the part of the Latin Fathers, since they would naturally translate ὑπόστασις not as "Person" but as "Substance," and so frequently misunderstand the Greek definitions of the Trinity as one οὐσία in three ὑποστάσεις and of Christ as two φύσεις in one ὑπόστασις.

For a detailed treatment, see A. Michel, "Hypostase" in *Dict. Théol. Cath.* 7.369–437; and G. L. Prestige, *God in Patristic Thought* (London 1936).

[77] Cf. John 16.28.
[78] Cf. *ibid.* 15.26.
[79] Cf. John 1.14, 18 (see also *ibid.* 3.16, 18; Heb. 11.17; 1 John 4.9).
[80] Rom. 8.9.
[81] 2 Cor. 3.17.
[82] See above, n. 69.
[83] Ps. 79.3.
[84] Mark 2.7.
[85] στοιχεῖα, the four elements—fire, water, air, and earth—which the ancients believed to be the components of the human body.
[86] For Christ as our physician, always a popular concept with the Fathers and so employed already by Ignatius of Antioch (*Ephes.* 7.2), cf. the note by J. C. Plumpe, ACW 5.190 f.
[87] Cf. Ps. 113.12 (Sept.).
[88] Most of the earlier Greek Fathers teach a semi-material angelic nature. So e. g. Clement of Alexandria, *Exc. ex Theodot.* 11, speaks about their σώματα... εὔμορφα καὶ νοερά ("bodies ... comely and spiritual"); Hippolytus, *Ref. haer.* 10.33, thinks their bodies are of fire; Methodius, *De resurr.* 2.30.8, assumes that they are of pure air and fire; Basil, *De Spir. Sanct.* 38, basing himself on the authority of Ps. 103.4, also considers them to have bodies of πῦρ ἄϋλον ("immaterial fire"). Gregory of Nazianzus, *Orat.* 38.9, is not sure whether they are purely "intellectual spirits," νοερὰ πνεύματα, or "immaterial fire, as it were—fire without body," whereas Eusebius, *Dem. Ev.* 4.5.12, speaks of them as "intellectual and reasonable substances"; and Theodoret, *Quaest. in Gen.* 1.20, is quite explicit: "Angels and archangels, and all the bodiless and holy natures that are totally devoid of bodies and possess absolute invisibility." The authority of Pseudo-Dionysius finally established the perfect immateriality of angels. In the present passage they seem to be considered as purely spiritual; if Gregory speaks of ethereal places, he evidently uses metaphorical language; see for this Daniélou, *op. cit.* 160 ff.
[89] ἀποκατάστασις, a much-discussed word, since Origen used it and its verb to signify the restoration of all creatures (ἀποκ. πάντων), including the damned and the devils, to communion with God; cf. *De princ.* 2.10.8; 3.6.3; *C. Cels.* 8.72; *Schol. in Luc.* 14.20 (MG 17.364D); etc. Cf. C. Lenz, "Apokatastasis," *Reallex. f. Ant. u. Christ.* 1 (1950) 514–16. The teaching was anathema-

tized by the Synod of Constantinople in 543. Gregory appears to have held the doctrine—cf. e. g. the *oratio catechetica* 26, where he speaks of an ἀποκατάστασις τῶν νῦν ἐν κακίᾳ κειμένων; *De hom. opif.* 17; *De an. et resurr.* 72B; etc. He is accused of teaching it by Anastasius Sinaita, *Hodegos* 22 (MG 89.289D). In the present passage, however, the term may be taken to imply no more than the General Resurrection. See E. Michaud, "St. Grégoire de Nysse et l'apocatastase," *Rev. internat. théol.* 10 (1902) 37–52; J. Daniélou, "L'apocatastase chez saint Grégoire de Nysse," *Rech. sc. rel.* 30 (1940) 328–47; for Gregory, see Leys, *op. cit.* 88–92.

⁹⁰ 1 Thess. 4.17.

⁹¹ καλὸν κἀγαθόν. The well-known classical term was first applied to man, denoting in Aristotle the morally perfect, and then also to things and to the idea of moral perfection. Gregory, like other classically trained Fathers, applies it to Christian morality.

⁹² Cf. Col. 1.16; also Eph. 1.21 and 3.10.

⁹³ φιλοσοφία; its root meaning, *love* or *pursuit of wisdom*, rather than *philosophy* in the technical sense of the term (in which it is used by the Fathers almost exclusively for pagan philosophy), is the foundation of the main Patristic uses of the word. In the present passage it has preserved the sense of *doctrine, teaching*, since for the Fathers the Christian teaching is the φιλοσοφία *par excellence*. The word is defined as "understanding . . . of being and of true knowledge" by Justin Martyr, *Dial.* 3.3, who likes to couple it with εὐσέβεια ("piety"), e. g. *1 Apol.* 3.2, and asserts that Christianity has the only true philosophy— so *Dial.* 8.1. With the rise of monasticism it came to be especially associated with the moral and ascetical life, which is frequently simply called φιλοσοφία—so by Gregory himself in his *Vita Macrinae* (MG 46.960C), to give but one example from his works, and throughout the ascetical literature.

⁹⁴ Cf. Matt. 13.3 ff.; Mark 4.3 ff.; Luke 8.5 ff.

⁹⁵ δι' αἰνιγμάτων. The Christian use of the word αἴνιγμα, which in classical Greek meant especially *dark saying, riddle*, derives from the famous passage in First Corinthians 13.12, "We see now through a glass, *in a dark manner* (ἐν αἰνίγματι)," where it denotes the knowledge of Divine things in the darkness of faith as opposed to the perfect knowledge in heaven "face to face"—πρόσωπον πρὸς πρόσωπον. As faith-knowledge comes to us largely in symbols, αἴνιγμα later acquired this sense, being

also often applied, as in the present passage, to the metaphorical language of the Old Testament, as well as to its types as opposed to the full truth of the New Testament, so e. g. Gregory in *De an. et resurr.* (MG 46.132B). This latter meaning is particularly frequent in writers of the Alexandrian school, so constantly in Cyril, e. g. *Hom. Pasch.* 16.4 (MG 77.756B): "The Law is the pedagogue, which guides us to the better understanding by symbols (δι' αἰνιγμάτων)"; see also Olympiodorus, *In Ier.* 23.9 (MG 93.676B), etc.

[96] In the Bible βίος is generally reserved to the animal life or the span of man's life on earth, ζωή more often to the eternal or the spiritual life. In the Fathers this distinction is also made, but not without many exceptions. In the present passage the two kinds of life are evidently opposed, though elsewhere Gregory uses the words sometimes interchangeably. Wherever βίος and ζωή are used with their original distinctive meaning, ζωή is translated as *spiritual life, life of the soul,* etc., βίος as *animal life, material life,* etc., according to the sense of the passage.

[97] It is difficult to reproduce what is probably a play on the word ἁρμονία, which can mean both "*chink*" and *harmony,* and ἁρμόνιος, which means *harmonious, balanced, well-fitted.*

[98] Gen. 3.15 (Sept., but with the objects interchangeable).

[99] *Ibid.* 3.19.

[100] Ps. 103.14.

[101] Cf. *ibid.* 146.9.

[102] *Ibid.* 135.25.

[103] *Ibid.* 144.16.

[104] Lit., "benefactor (promoter) of iniquity"—τοῦ εὐεργέτου τῆς ἀδικίας. *Euergetes* was an honorary title popular in the Hellenistic period not only for gods and rulers, but also for philosophers, inventors, physicians, etc. Philo uses the term indiscriminately for God and emperor. In the New Testament (Luke 22.25 f.) the title belongs to God (Christ) alone, not to man. Cf. G. Bertram, "εὐεργετέω, etc.," Kittel's *Theol. Wörterb. z. N. T.* 2 (1935) 651 f.

[105] Cf. 2 Cor. 6.15.

[106] Isa. 1.11, 13.

[107] Cf. *ibid.* 66.3.

[108] φιλοσοφία—cf. above, n. 93.

[109] Prov. 27.1.

[110] Matt. 6.34.

[111] *Ibid.* 6.33 f.

[112] ὀφειλήματα means both moral trespasses and material debts, as the Latin *debita.* We have translated *debts* because else the play on words in what follows would have been untranslatable.

[113] Cf. Luke 5.21.

[114] Cf. above, nn. 26 and 44, and Merki, *op. cit.* 133–35.

[115] 1 Cor. 4.16; 11.1.

[116] Cf. Luke 15.8.

[117] Cf. *ibid.* 15.11 ff.

[118] Cf. *ibid.* 12.33 (?).

[119] Matt. 19.20; Luke 18.21.

[120] Covetousness is idolatry: cf. Col. 3.5.

[121] Referring to John the Baptist—cf. Matt. 11.11 (Luke 7.28) and Luke 1.17.

[122] Apparently a reminiscence of Prov. 24.16 or Eccles. 7.21, or both.

[123] Cf. above, n. 43.

[124] Turning to the East was the ordinary attitude of prayer in the ancient Church. The mystical reason here given is reproduced elsewhere, e. g. Basil, *De Spir. Sancto* 27.66; Chrysostom, *Comm. in Dan.* 6.10; Ps.-Athanasius, *Quaest. ad Antiochum* 37 (MG 28.620AB), where another reason is added, namely, that the light, a symbol of God, rises in the East. Cf. F. J. Dölger, *Sol Salutis, Gebet und Gesang im christlichen Altertum mit besonderer Rücksicht auf die Ostung in Gebet und Liturgie* (2. ed. Münster i. W. 1925) *passim.*

[125] Gen. 2.8 (Sept.).

[126] 1 Cor. 15.22.

[127] Cf. Eph. 2.5.

[128] Jer. 9.21.

[129] Mark 7.21; Matt. 15.19.

[130] Prov. 20.9 (Sept.).

[131] Job 14.4 (Sept.).

[132] ἡδονή is generally used for the pleasure of the senses, whereas χαρά is reserved to denote spiritual joy. ἡδονή was also the name of an Aeon in the Gnostic system—cf. Irenaeus, *Adv. haer.* 1.1.3 (Mass.). For the meaning of the word in the New Testament, and its prehistory, see G. Stählin, "ἡδονή," in Kittel, *Theol. Wörterb. z. N. T.* 2 (1935) 911–28.

[133] Luke 4.23.

[134] ἐν εὐκτηρίῳ, lit. "place of prayer," "oratory"; εὐκτήριον here

to be distinguished from εὐκτήριος οἶκος: "public" and "private" oratory. The "public" oratories were the smaller churches in town or country (as compared with the larger churches or basilicas in the cities), while "private" oratories were found in hospices (ξενοδοχεῖα), the homes of bishops and high public officials. The Emperor Constantine, for example, had a portable oratory or chapel on his military campaigns: Eusebius, *Vita Const.* 2.127, etc. Cf. H. Leclercq, "Oratoire," *Dict. d'archéol. chrét. et de lit.* 12.2 (1936) 2346–72, esp. 60 f.

[135] Cf. Matt. 18.23 ff.

[136] Ps. 8.8 f.

[137] *Ibid.* 146.9 (cf. 103.14).

[138] 1 John 5.19–therefore not a Gospel word as seems implied.

THE BEATITUDES

[1] Here, as elsewhere in Gregory's writings (cf. below, Serm. 3 —p. 110 ff. and n. 37; *In Ps.* 7: MG 44.453B; etc.), there is an obvious reminiscence of the celebrated allegory of the Cave of Plato, *De rep.* 514–16. Cf. Cherniss, *The Platonism of Gregory of Nyssa* 44, 85 f.

[2] Isa. 2.3.

[3] Cf. *ibid.* 35.3.

[4] Cf. *ibid.* 53.4 (Matt. 8.17).

[5] On Gregory's conception of man's restoration to the image of God (cf. above, n. 8 to the *De Or. Dom.*) through the coming of Christ and the institution of baptism, cf. Merki, *op. cit.* 161 f.

[6] Cf. Matt. 6.19 f.

[7] ἡ πρὸς τὸ Θεῖον ὁμοίωσις: cf. above, n. 44 to the *De Or. Dom.*; also Merki, *op. cit.* 109.

[8] Cf. 1 Tim. 6.15.

[9] 2 Cor. 8.9.

[10] Phil. 2.5–7.

[11] These are not mentioned in the Gospel narrative of the Nativity, but are accommodations based on Isaias (1.3: *The ox knoweth his owner, and the ass his master's crib*) and Habacuc (1.3). Because the Fathers often interpreted the "irrational beasts" mentioned in Isaias allegorically—the ox for the Jewish people and the ass for the Gentiles—it is difficult to say when the tradition arose that these animals were also historically present at the Nativity. In the present passage this tradition seems to be implied. From the beginning of the 4th century the animals appear on a number of pictorial representations of the Nativity, notably on sarcophagi: cf. H. Leclercq, "Ane," *Dict. d'archéol. chrét. et de lit.* 1.2 (1924) 2047–2059.

[12] Cf. Lev. 18.6 ff.

[13] Matt. 19.21.

[14] *Ibid.* 19.27.

[15] Cf. 1 Thess. 4.16.

[16] Ps. 111.9.

[17] 1 Cor. 2.9, citing Isa. 64.4.

¹⁸ Ps. 26.13.

¹⁹ Cf. Ps. 86.3, whence (cf. also *ibid.* 45.4, 47.2, 3) St. Augustine borrowed the title for his greatest work—cf. *De civ. Dei* 11.1.

²⁰ 1 Thess. 4.16.

²¹ πραότης, meekness, with a secondary meaning of slowness, sedateness; the following exegesis attempts to do justice to both these senses, though the obvious meaning of the passage is sometimes obscured by this double interpretation.

²² 1 Cor. 9.24.

²³ Cf. *ibid.* 9.27.

²⁴ Cf. Gal. 6.17.

²⁵ Cf. Ps. 17.37 f.

²⁶ Cf. Cant. 2.9, 8.

²⁷ Cf. John 15.1.

²⁸ Cf. n. 3 on the Sermons on the Lord's Prayer.

²⁹ Cf. n. 68 *ibid.*

³⁰ Heb. 12.1.

³¹ Cf. 2 Cor. 7.10. For the concept of sorrow, mourning —πένθος—in the Fathers of the East (John Chrysostom wrote a treatise on the subject—MG 47.393–422), cf. J. Hausherr, *Penthos: la doctrine de la componction dans l'Orient chrétien* (Orientalia Christiana Analecta 132, Rome 1944); for Gregory of Nyssa, *passim.*

³² Cf. Eph. 2.1, 4.18 f.; Col. 2.13.

³³ Cf. Matt. 8.12, 22.13, 30; Mark 9.43; Luke 13.28; etc.

³⁴ 2 Cor. 2.7; cf. 1 Cor. 5.1–5 for the grievous sin probably referred to here.

³⁵ A play on words, Παράκλητος (the Paraclete) and παρακληθήσονται occurring in the Beatitude quoted again in the following sentence.

³⁶ Hab. 3.19.

³⁷ See above, n. 1, and Cherniss, *op. cit.* 85.

³⁸ See above, n. 8 on The Lord's Prayer; Merki, *op. cit.* 139.

³⁹ Cf. Exod. 12.8.

⁴⁰ See n. 57 on The Lord's Prayer.

⁴¹ See n. 96 *ibid.*

⁴² Ps. 119.5.

⁴³ See *ibid.* 83.

⁴⁴ Luke 16.25.

⁴⁵ Cf. Ps. 83.6.

⁴⁶ Matt. 4.3.

[47] Cf. *ibid.* 4.4 (Deut. 8.3).

[48] John 4.34.

[49] 1 Tim. 2.4.

[50] A conflation of Exod. 3.5 and Isa. 42.8.

[51] Exod. 3.14.

[52] *Ibid.* 22.27.

[53] Cf. Prov. 23.27.

[54] Ps. 41.3.

[55] *Ibid.* 16.15.

[56] Cf. Hab. 3.3.

[57] Cf. Ps. 33.9.

[58] John 14.23.

[59] Gal. 2.20.

[60] Cf. Phil. 3.13.

[61] *Ibid.* 3.12.

[62] Cf. Gen. 28.12.

[63] θεοποιέω, make Divine, a term frequently used with reference to Christians, whom God has raised to a superhuman state; so e. g. Origen, *De or.* 27.13, and especially Athanasius, who coined the famous phrase "He became man, so that we might be made god"—*De Incarn.* 54.3.

[64] Ps. 114.5.

[65] 1 Cor. 12.31.

[66] Luke 17.21.

[67] Matt. 7.8.

[68] This passage is directed against the dualistic heresies of the times, Gnosis and Manicheism, which believed in a good and an evil principle.

[69] Rom. 2.7 f.

[70] The metaphor of the mirror is a favourite of the Greek Fathers, frequently used of the soul reflecting the Image of God, so e. g. Athanasius, *Contra gent.* 34, and by Gregory himself in the 6th sermon of this treatise, a passage quite similar to the Athanasian one. Cf. also his 7th Sermon on the Canticle (PG 44.920C). It seems that Daniélou, *Platonisme et Théologie Mystique* 228, where he states that the image of the mirror *est bien proprement Grégorienne au sens où notre nature le prend,* was unaware of the Athanasius passage, which would seem to have inspired the later writer.

[71] Matt. 25.34, 41.

[72] 2 Cor. 6.14.

[73] Gal. 6.8.

[74] A favourite idea of Gregory: cf. *The Lord's Prayer*, Sermon 5.

[75] Matt. 25.34 ff.

[76] *Ibid.* 25.40.

[77] Luke 16.25.

[78] John 1.18.

[79] 1 Tim. 6.16.

[80] Cf. Exod. 33.20.

[81] Ps. 127.5.

[82] Isa. 26.10 (Sept.).

[83] Cf. 1 John 4.12.

[84] 2 Tim. 4.8.

[84a] Cf. John 13.23, 21.20.

[85] Cf. Exod. 33.17.

[86] Rom. 11.33.

[87] Ps. 103.24.

[88] The ἐνέργειαι of God, as distinct from the Divine Persons, are, according to Greek theology, certain Divine operations, such as sanctifying grace, which establish a connection between the inaccessible Divinity and the created world. This conception, which is quite foreign to Western theology, is noticeable already in Basil, Gregory, and other earlier Fathers. It was later elaborated especially by Gregory Palamas. See V. Lossky, *Essai sur la théologie mystique de l'Église d'Orient* (Paris 1944) chapter on *Energies incrées*, 65 ff.

[89] For the theology of the "senses of the soul," which was developed already by Origen, see Daniélou, *op. cit.* pp. 237 ff.

[90] Luke 17.21.

[91] Cf. n. 70.

[92] Cf. Matt. 5.21 f.

[93] *Ibid.* Many Biblical manuscripts and Fathers (Justin, Origen, etc.) add εἰκῇ (*sine causa*), "in vain," after "brother."

[94] Num. 25.6 f.

[95] Cf. Exod. 26.1 ff.

[96] See n. 55 on *The Lord's Prayer*.

[97] Gen. 18.27.

[98] Isa. 40.6.

[99] Ps. 36.2.

[100] Eccles. 1.2.

[101] Cf. 1 Cor. 15.9.

[102] Cf. Isa. 40.12.

[103] Cf. *ibid.* 40.25 (18, 46.5).

[104] Eccles. 5.1.

[105] θεωρία, consideration or contemplation. The term was used for the visions of the O. T. prophets, and hence, according to H. de Lubac, "Typologie et allégorisme," *Rech. de Sc. Rel.* 34 (1947) 202, applied to the higher or "mystical" sense of Scripture. It is so used from Origen onwards throughout the Patristic period, side by side with its original meaning of contemplation.

[106] ἀγάπη, the general term for Christian love, used more frequently than ἔρως, though without altogether replacing it. See my article, "Eros et Agapé," in *Vie Spir.* Suppl. 4 (1949/50) 99–105.

[107] Cf. Gal. 5.22.

[108] A reference to the dualistic heresies, e. g. Gnosticism, Manicheism.

[109] Cf. the superscriptions to Psalms 6 and 11.

[110] Cf. n. 43 on *The Lord's Prayer.*

[111] Matt. 25.32 ff.

[112] Rom. 8.29 f.

[113] Heb. 4.12.

[114] Something seems to have gone wrong with the text here; for St. Paul, as a Roman citizen, was beheaded, not crucified, and Peter was not crucified head downwards. It is equally strange that Paul, James, and Stephen should be named before Peter. I suggest reading Peter for Paul, and Andrew for Peter, which would bring the passage in line with tradition and preserve the proper order of names.

[115] John 8.34.

[116] Heb. 12.11.

[117] Cf. 1 Cor. 9.24.

INDEX

INDEX

Aaron, 185
Abel, 164, 183
Abraham, 115, 155
Adam, 13; disobedience of, 41, 76 f., 183
ἄδυτον, 46 f., 154, 185; see Holy of Holies
ἀγάπη, 198; see charity
αἴνιγμα, 190 f. See symbols
Alexandrian theology, 8, 181, 191
allegorical (mystical) exegesis, 6, 7; cf. 159, 185, 194, 198
Amalecites, 24
Ambrose, 182
Amphilochius, 179
Anastasius Sinaita, Hodegos 22: 190
Andrew, St., 198
angelic life, of Christian, 50, 63; in Paradise, 138
angels, helpers in the battle against evil, 52; their nature, 61, 189; exempt from bodily needs, 63; opposed to brute creation, 138
Anthony, St., 16
Antioch, Synod of (379), 4
ἀπάθεια, ἀπαθής, 52, 63, 180, 182, 187; see passions
ἀποκατάστασις, 6, 189 f.
Apollinarianism, 5
Arianism, 4, 5, 187
Aristotle, 188, 190
ἁρμονία, 191
Assyrians, 24

Asterius Amasenus, Hom. 10: 183
Athanasius, 3
  C. gent. 34: 196; De Incarn. 54.3: 196; De virg. 1: 187; Exp. fid. 2: 188; Exp. Ps. 111.5: 182; [Quaest. ad Antioch.] 37: 192; Tom. ad Antioch. 5: 188
Augustine, 19, 195
  De civ. Dei 11.1: 195

Backer, E. de, 186
baptism, 185, 186, 194
Bardy, G., 187
Basil, 3, 5, 7
  De Spir. Sanct. 27.66: 192; 38: 189; 75: 182; Ep. 38: 188; 235.6: 188; [In Isa.] prooem. 3: 185
βασιλεία, 11, 187; see Kingdom of God, kingship
βατταλογέω, 27 f., 181
Baus, K., 181
Beatific Vision, 17, 144
beatitude, defined, 87; God its ground, 130; attained by men through mercy, 131; opposed to riches, 140, 144
Beelzebub, 83
Belial, 68
Bertram, G., 191
βίος, 115, 191; see life
body, part of human being, 61; its needs, 64, 184
Bornkamm, G., 186

but can be possessed and contemplated by the pure soul, 17, 150; ways of knowing Him, 146 ff.; self-existing, 112; simple, 165; impassible, 31; unchangeable, 50; His lovingkindness, 32, 82; Divine names, 38, 125, 153; His holiness, 48; Kingship, 50 f., 73; justice, 67; beatitude, 87; His Fatherhood does not extend to unrepentant sinner, 38 ff.; how to be imitated by man, 71 ff., 90

grace, 16, 19, 77, 154; sanctifying, 197; as food and drink, 124

Graef, H. C., 185, 198

Gregory of Nazianzus, 3, 4
   Ep. 107: 179; *Orat.* 38.9: 189; 39.11: 188; 40.31: 185

Gregory of Nyssa, neglected by scholars, 3; married, 3; ascetical life, 4; lack of firmness, 4; archbishop of Sebaste, 4; eschatological teaching, 5; as ascetical and mystical writer, 6, 16; influence of Origen, 6, 16; characteristics of his writings, 7; mystical theology, 7; exegesis, 8; Trinitarian teaching, 8 ff.; personality, 19 f.; The Lord's Prayer, 7 ff., compared with other treatises on the subject, 10; The Beatitudes, 6 f., 16; other works, 5 ff.
   C. Eunom. 2 (vulg.) 13: 188; 11 (Jaeger 2.270.13):

185; *De an. et resurr.* MG 46.72B: 190; 132B: 191; 148C: 184; *De bapt. Christi* MG 46.581A: 185; 584C: 182; *De hom. opif.* 16: 181; 17: 190; *De virg.* 3: 179; 12: 181, 183; *De vita Moys.* MG 44.317A, C: 182; 376 ff.: 182; *Ep.* 13: 179; *In Cant.* hom. 1: 186; hom. 7: 196; hom. 15: 179; *In Ps.* 7: 194; *Or. Catech.* 6: 183; 26: 190; 33: 186; 34: 185; *Vita Macrinae* MG 46.960C: 190

groat, loss of, 75

Habacuc, 109, 129

Hausherr, J., 195

health, 17, 57, 60, 139, 148, 173; of the soul, 58; physical and spiritual, 117 f.

Heaven, true home of man, 42, 44, 62, 97, 145, 150, 174

hell, 108, 141 f., 153

Hippolytus, *Ref. haer.* 10.33: 189

Holl, K., 8 f., 179

Holy of Holies, 7, 45 ff., 154, 185

hope, 34, 69, 144, 170

Horn, G., 179

Hort, F. J. A., 187

humility, natural to human condition, 90; mother of meekness, 104; opposed to wrath, 105

hypocrisy, 162

idolatry, twofold, of idols and of greed, 59, 75, 192

Theaet. 17ab: 184
pleasure, transitory, 126; sins of, healed by Christ, 152; 192
Plotinus, 18, 188
 Enn. 1.2.1: 184; 5: 188
Plumpe, J. C., 189
πνεῦμα (Χριστοῦ), 9
Pneumatomachi, 187
Pontus, 4
Poukens, J., 186
poverty, twofold, 89; of spirit, 90; of God, 91; voluntary, 95; not to be feared, 96
πραότης, 195; see meekness
prayer, need for, 7; science of, 21; prevents sin, 23; confidence in, 36, 38, 43, 71 ff., 82, 182; place of, 192 f.; effects of, 24; of petition, 28; see also vow
Prestige, G. L., 188
pride, 90 ff.; produces wrath, 104; see also vanity
Prodigal Son, parable of, 41 f., 75, 77
προσεύχομαι, προσευχή, 36 f., 183; see prayer, vow
πρόσωπον, 190
Psalmist, 30 f., 129
Ps.-Dionysius, 186, 189
 De div. nom. 2.7: 186; *De myst. theol.* 1.1: 186
Pulcheria, 5
purification, 35; activity of the H. Spirit and of Christ, 53; effects, 148, 166; by suffering, 172
purity, 18, 38; of conscience, 40; given by Christ, 45; angelic, 63; defiled by sensual

pleasure, 79; of heart, 144 ff.; how to be achieved, 151 ff.; see chastity

Quasten, J., 182

reason, opposed to passions, 103; its absence in animals, 114
Resurrection, 166, 190
retribution, 13 f., 137
riches, 86; two kinds of, 89
rich young man, 75

sacraments, 186
sacramentum, 186; see mysteries
Samaritan woman, 124
Samuel, 77
Scripture, allegorical interpretation of, 185
senses, their pleasures transitory, 64, 126; causes of sin, 65, 78; of pleasure, 171; of the soul, 148, 150, 197
serpent, 42; as symbol of lust, 65 f., 77
Seth, 183
Sifanus, 20
sin, 11, 13, 15, 23, 71, etc.; reasons for its ubiquity, 22, 108; its forgiveness a Divine activity, 56; its introduction into human nature, 58; done easily, 60; separates from God, 72, 74; universal, 78 f.; in relation to the Image, 88; its transmission, 151
Solomon, 139
sonship, man's Divine, 10, 154, 156